'Ben Okri has a conception of what art and literature are and the larger place they should play in society ... Okri imbues these essays with a writer's insight about the importance of writing – and he does so in an inimitably sinuous yet abstract style well suited to his theme ... oblique, oneiric, rhapsodic, elliptical'   *Independent on Sunday*

'I defy you not to try it'   *Independent*

'There can be no mistaking Okri's passion and intelligence. He sees the role of the writer, his main concern in these pieces, as that of liberator, witness and explorer of hidden depths. The most interesting essay in the book is about *Othello* ... the essay remains a powerful piece of work. It deserves a permanent place in the literature of *Othello*'
Sunday Telegraph

'Okri is marvellously enthusiastic at promoting the poetic cause, pouring out his love for creativity in The Joys Of Storytelling with a passionate reverence'   *Daily Express*

'Okri's writing is thoughtful, concise, cultivated and clear'
Scotland on Sunday

'Okri is interesting, too, as an example of the extraordinary receptiveness of British or English culture; of its willingness to reach out to, and be enriched by, those coming from other traditions. Okri is at once as foreign and as British as Joseph Conrad'   *Daily Telegraph*

ALSO BY BEN OKRI

Fiction

Flowers and Shadows
The Landscapes Within
Incidents at the Shrine
Stars of the New Curfew
The Famished Road
Songs of Enchantment
Astonishing the Gods
Dangerous Love

Non-fiction

Birds of Heaven

Poetry

An African Elegy

Ben Okri has published many books including *The Famished Road*, which won the Booker Prize in 1991, *Songs of Enchantment, Astonishing the Gods* and *Dangerous Love*. He has also published a book of poems, *An African Elegy*. He has been a Fellow Commoner in Creative Arts, at Trinity College, Cambridge and he is a Fellow of the Royal Society of Literature.

Ben Okri's books have won several awards including the Commonwealth Writers Prize for Africa, the *Paris Review* Aga Khan Prize for Fiction, the Chianti Rufino-Antico Fattore International Literary Prize and the Premio Grinzane Cavour Prize. The World Economic Forum presented Ben Okri with the Crystal Award for his outstanding contribution to the Arts and to cross-cultural understanding. In addition, the University of Westminster awarded him an Honorary Doctorate of Literature. He is one of the Vice Presidents of the English Centre of International P.E.N. Ben Okri was born in Nigeria and now lives in London.

A Way of Being Free

BEN OKRI

PHŒNIX

A PHOENIX PAPERBACK

First published in Great Britain by Phoenix House in 1997
This paperback edition published in 1998 by Phoenix,
a division of Orion Books Ltd,
Orion House, 5 Upper St Martin's Lane,
London WC2H 9EA

A CIP catalogue record for this book
is available from the British Library.

ISBN: 0 75380 141 8

Printed and bound in Great Britain by
The Guernsey Press Co. Ltd, Guernsey, Channel Islands

To my brothers,
Andrew and Godwin Okri

CONTENTS

WHILE THE WORLD SLEEPS

'The poet is he who inspires far more
than he who is inspired.'

Paul Eluard

I

The world in which the poet lives does not necessarily
yield up the poetic. In the hands of the poet, the
world is resistant. It is only with the searching and the
moulding that the unyielding world becomes transformed in a new medium of song and metaphor.

It is not surprising therefore that poets seem to be
set against the world. The poet needs to be up at night,
when the world sleeps; needs to be up at dawn, before
the world wakes; needs to dwell in odd corners, where
Tao is said to reside; needs to exist in dark places, where
spiders forge their webs in silence; near the gutters,
where the underside of our dreams fester. Poets need
to live where others don't care to look, and they need
to do this because if they don't they can't sing to us of
all the secret and public domains of our lives. They

need to be multiple witnesses around the central masquerades of reality in order to convey fully the unimaginable dimensions of the deity's terrible and enchanting dance.

The great tidal crowds of everyday events pour in one direction, sometimes the poet has to move in the other – often moving directly against them, at other times cutting tangentially across the morning waves of humanity. Poets seem to be set against the world because we need them to show us the falseness of our limitations, the true extent of our kingdom.

The poet turns the earth into mother, the sky becomes a shelter, the sun an inscrutable god, and the pragmatists are irritated. They want the world to come with only one name, one form. The antagonists of poets and other transformers are those who refuse to see the fluid nature of reality, who cannot perceive that each individual reality is different. Laws do not bind our perceptions. There are as many worlds as there are lives. It is not those who have no imagination who are the problem, for we all possess imagination, few of us use it well. The problem is with those who are frightened of the rather limitless validity of the imagination, frightened of people who continually extend the boundaries of the possible, people who ceaselessly redream the world and reinvent existence; frontiers people of the unknown and the uncharted.

———

The enemies of poets are those who have no genuine religious thinking. To be truly religious does not require an institution, it requires terror, faith, compassion, imagination, and a belief in more than three dimensions. It also requires love. Religion touches us at the place where imagination blends into the divine. Poetry touches us where religion is inseparable from the wholly human. In heaven there could be no poetry. The same is true of hell. It is only on a sphere where heaven and hell are mixed into the fabric of the mortal frame that poetry is possible.

Poets are set against the world because they cannot accept that what there seems to be is all there is. Elias Canetti wrote once that: 'The inklings of poets are the forgotten adventures of God.' Poets are not the unacknowledged legislators of the world. They come with no tablets of stone, and they do not speak with God. They speak to us. Creation speaks to them. They listen. They remake the world in words, from dreams. Intuitions which could only come from the secret mouths of gods whisper to them through all of life, of nature, of visible and invisible agencies. Storms speak to them. Thunder breathes on them. Human suffering drives them. Flowers move their pens. Words themselves speak to them and bring forth more words. The poet is the widener of consciousness. The poet suffers our agonies as well and combines them with all the forgotten waves of childhood. Out of the mouths of poets speak the yearnings of our lives.

The acknowledged legislators of the world take the world as given. They dislike mysteries, for mysteries cannot be coded, or legislated, and wonder cannot be made into law. And so these legislators police the accepted frontiers of things. Politicians, heads of state, kings, religious leaders, soldiers, the rich, the powerful – they all fancy themselves the masters of this earthly kingdom. They speak to us of facts, policies, statistics, programmes, abstract and severe moralities. But the dreams of the people are beyond them, and would trouble them. The hard realities of the people would alarm them. It is they who have to curb the poet's vision of reality. It is they who invoke the infamous 'poetic licence' whenever they do not want to face the inescapable tragedy contained in, for example, Okigbo's words: 'I have lived the oracle dry on the cradle of a new generation.' It is they who demand that poetry be partisan, that it takes sides, usually their side; that it rides on the back of causes and issues, their causes, their issues, whoever they may be.

Our lives have become narrow enough. Our dreams strain to widen them, to bring to our waking consciousness the awareness of greater discoveries that lie just beyond the limits of our sights. We must not force our poets to limit the world any further. That is a crime against life itself. If the poet begins to speak only of narrow things, of things that we can effortlessly digest and recognise, of things that do not disturb, frighten, stir, or annoy us, or make us restless for more, make us cry for greater justice, make us want to set sail and explore inklings murdered in our youths, if the poet sings only of our restricted angles and in restricted terms and in restricted language, then what hope is there for any of us in this world?

Those of us who want this are cowards, in flesh and in spirit. We fear heroic heights. We dread the recombining of the world, dread a greater harvest of being. We sit lazily and demand that our poets draw the horizon closer. We therefore become separated from our true selves. Then even beauty can seem repugnant. Then, we no longer recognise who we are, and we forget what we used to be, what states we sometimes inhabited, what extended moments of awareness. It is those who are scared of reality, of their own truths, of their own histories, those who are secretly sickened by what they have become, who are alarmed by the strange mask-like faces that peer back at them from the mirrors of time, it is they who resist the poetic. They resist the poetic with all their hidden might because if they don't, the power of words speaking in their own heads would burst open their inner doors, and all the monsters breeding within would come bounding out and crashing on the floors of their consciousness. What would hold their inner frames together then? They have to suppress the poetic, or accept it only on blurred terms, or promote its cruder imitations, for the simple reason that they have long ago begun suppressing eruptive life and all its irreconcilable shadings, its natural paradoxes.

The antagonists of poetry cannot win. The world seems resistant but carries within it for ever the desire to be transformed into something higher. The world may seem unyielding but, like invisible forces in the air, it merely awaits imagination and will to unloosen the magic within itself. The poet is not a creator but an alchemist. Poets are helplessly on the side of the greatest good, the highest causes, the most just future.

And because they are helplessly on the side of the future it may be valid to say that they need their antagonists. Poets need to be kept alive and awake. We should beware the hardening arteries of our lives. That is perhaps why prophets speak out with such incandescent, irrepressible concern at what we are doing to ourselves. In that sense all prophets have something of the poet, though not all poets are prophets.

The poet as quantum physicist, as healer, as angel and demon of the word cannot afford to disdain the world, cannot feel superior to it any more than the scientist can feel superior to thunder, to mountains, or to the constellations. There are no superiorities of function, only ascendencies.

Their love shows in the quality of their dreams and their works. The deeper poets feel, the deeper is their exploration. The more we want to reconnect, the more we would follow poets in their quest for impossible transformations. They measure the heroism of the consciousness of any age. It is true when they say that poets are never ahead of their times. It is only we who are far behind ours.

2

Hunger is an antagonist. Different kinds of hunger. Society can be defined as the sphere in which all our hungers meet, as in a great chaotic marketplace. The poet's hunger is our hunger, which is for more life. We all feel that terrible pull sometimes. We are all being herded down, tricked along, illusory highways which seem to lead nowhere, except only to the grave. Did we choose our roads? Did our roads choose us? Did we arrive on them by proxy?

We all feel that pull sometimes, the pull that connects us to Dante's 'love that moves the sun and stars'. And sometimes it comes when we are least prepared, when we are naked, asleep. It comes in silence. It comes in the dead of night. It comes like Rilke's armies of reality, the armies that besiege 'undisturbed cities', the ones that lie 'outside the walls like a countryside', and who 'send no one into the city to threaten/or promise, and no one to negotiate'. Yes, sometimes it comes at night. And we awake, sweating. We do not know what has awoken us. Why have we awoken? What has caused this disturbance of our sleep?

We get out of bed. We wander round the house, to see if everything is all right. Nothing stirs. Everything sleeps. The world snores gently. We try to return to sleep, but the question nags us: why have we woken up? When was the last time we woke suddenly like this for no visible reason? And then gradually, if we are lucky, we realise that something seemingly silent in our lives is trying to speak to us. We realise that we have been woken for the strange and simple reason that our sleep should be disturbed. A great fear, or a great yearning, has been forming in us. We cannot tell when it began. We do not know how to deal with the undeciphered terror or fill the sudden emptiness, the foreboding. We may have become aware over the last few days that the sky has been slowly eclipsed by the accumulation of our daily worries, or our deadening habits. Human faces might have been increasingly taking on the polarised forms of those who are for us or those who are against us. They seem more against us. We no longer see the world. We've stopped looking. We no longer marvel at something beautiful. We've stopped noticing. We can't really remember the last time we experienced the quickening of the unknown. The realisation drives away sleep. Something vaguely disconcerting is growing in us, occupying more space, like a sense of guilt freed suddenly from the shackles of our wilful forgetting. Then we might begin to suspect that somewhere, somehow, we took the wrong turning, went up the wrong road. It might have been a long time ago, in the midst of our confusion. We may now have travelled too far towards an undesired destination. And now, in the night, surrounded by the magnifying energies of silence, we look around and we don't recognise the road or the destination. When did we take the wrong turning? What road were we travelling on in the first place? After some reflection we suspect that it was a branching off from the unsignposted road of youth, that road lined with anxieties and promises, vague notions of a splendid future without too much work in which the world could have shone with a thousand pleasant colours, in which songs burned the heart with desire, in which our sensations flared brightly.

You turn on the bed: it feels rough. You wonder how you could ever sleep on the same bed, night after night. It feels a little like a limiter of your estate. You get up. You tread the house. The floor doesn't yield. The walls are solid – they don't look as if the armies of reality that Rilke wrote about could break them down in silence. But you look around your room with strange eyes. When did you settle into this? When did your abode become your shell? The house seems unfamiliar, as if it belonged to a stranger who had settled in hastily and never taken the trouble to live in it properly and enjoy all its possibilities. Your property, at this moment, looks as if it's all on loan. The house fairly rebukes you. The house, the room, has become your road. You wander deeper into its hidden disintegrations. Everywhere, all your dreams are fading, have faded. Photographs of you mock you with their fixity.

You make yourself a drink. Something stirs in you. Something seeps into your heart. And then, in an instant, without warning, you remember faces that have disappeared in the turnings you took to avoid being like them. You remember your early dreams, your youthful boasts. You remember those you no longer see. Where are they now? What has the world done to them?

You move in your chair. It creaks. Your life creaks under your weight, slowly giving up the ghost. You try to remember yourself in your best moments. The pictures are dim. The vanities of your triumphs fairly unsettle you with their relative insignificance. Viewing yourself now with the severity you usually reserve for others, you suddenly conceive a vague dislike of yourself. You wonder how you wound up the person you are. Attempting to rally some dignity, you repeat your achievements to yourself in a slightly pompous *sotto voce*. This doesn't improve the unease, the sitting sideways in yourself. Your achievements diminish as you name them. You ask yourself: what have I done that could outlive me, that could become more beautiful with the merciless clarification of time, that sits quietly in my soul, a further aid to greater deeds? You can't think of anything. You sigh. Something sinks in you. Something sad. You are overcome with the absurd notion that your life could be different. You're not sure how or in what way.

Your drink is definitely lukewarm. You begin to think of trivialities. Your mind, unwilling to face the full implications of the truth, takes the first byroad it can deceive you into. You wander down that road. You think of money. You think of something someone said yesterday, something small, but which stung your vanity a little. What did they mean by that remark anyway? You move again in your chair. You realise that your unease is slipping away from you. Your incomprehension is giving way to a petty state of recrimination. There you are, woken by a nameless yearning, a feeling which if followed to its naked conclusion could change your life: and now you begin to find being awake a little boring. I could think these thoughts in the morning, you say to yourself. And this nakedness, this feeling, which lurks at the roots of poetry, conversion, intuition, change – this deceptive gift of the spirit which does its best to warn you, to throw signs at you, is suppressed, eclipsed, by vanity. Saul Bellow was right when he wrote: 'It's too bad, but suffering is about the only reliable burster of the spirit's sleep.'

Your drink, meanwhile, has turned cold. You reach for your slippers. They slide from your toes' grasp. You look at them and somewhat forcefully shove your feet into them. You take the cup to the kitchen, satisfying a lower sense of order. You put the lights off in each room. Nothing feels so strange anymore. It all looks familiar. You recognise it all. You built it thus. You set it up thus. This is your life. It's better, you think, than the lives millions of people have. As you cross the sitting room you take in the symmetries of the place. Maybe I'll change the curtains, you say out loud. Or get some new carpets. Your eyes fall on the bookshelf. Another time, you think. You put out the light, feeling a little more unsettled in yourself, a little more at home, a little diminished, but you can't understand why.

It may be that what you *could be* haunts you. It is real. It is a weight you have to carry around. Each failure to become, to be, is a weight. Each state you could inhabit is a burden as heavy as any physical weight, but more so, because it weighs on your soul. It is the ghost of your possibilities hanging around your neck, an invisible albatross, potentials unknowingly murdered. The higher being you could *be*, if you could inhabit a higher state, also sits on you, increasing the tensions of your spirit, your moods, your irritations.

And so, feeling diminished, and having paradoxically gained a greater burden, you go to bed. But you don't sleep immediately. Repressed faces, forgotten words, replies you failed to deliver in a split second to someone's comment, dance round across your mind. In fact, that night you don't sleep soundly at all. That is how in secret moments we repress and deny the poetic. That is how we murder our dreams. Then we carry the suppression of the poetic into our waking lives and wreak our vengeance on the world. Having avoided a self-confrontation, and being more pompous in our waking hours for the self-diminishment of our secret ones, that is how we become the antagonist of poets – enemies of the widening of the world towards a vaster, more wondrous reality. That is how we narrow the world's sense of wonder. Antagonists of poets are among the life-haters, for whom Dante has a special place in a circle of the Inferno.

3

Poets sing for all the world in one breast. They sing for all those who need the unique nourishment of the poetic. Poets may choose to align themselves with the wretched and the voiceless of this planet. They may not. But they must draw to themselves heaven's aid, for their calling is absorbing and demanding, rigorous as conscience and elusive as freedom. They could, if they choose (and their choice is dictated by the quality of their love) breathe unease on complacency, stir the meek against injustice, help the blind to see, and, to appropriate what Pascal said about the parables of Christ, blind those who can see. Where there is misery they might be moved to soothe, to rouse, to sing of revolt, to spread hope and deeper dreams of liberation.

'For want of vision my people perish.' People die not only from hunger and famine, they die also from spiritual undernourishment, spiritual kwashiorkor, spiritual AIDS. For at any given time and place there are many inner selves to feed and we do not have enough good poets to feed us. 'There are many wand-bearers, but few inspired,' Socrates said. The poets that could be better than good, whose words breathe gusts of incandescent and higher oxygen over the lands, wage an unending battle against the antagonists within and without. Few of these poets come through a lifetime's struggle, their visions of hell, and can say in their works, like Homer's Odysseus, and with that fearful Delphic clarity: 'I have heard the songs of the sirens.'

Poets, be cunning. Learn some of the miracles. Survive. Weave your transformations in your life as well as in your work. Live. Stay alive. Don't go under, don't go mad, don't let them define you, or confine you, or buy your silence. If they do confine you, burst out of their prisons with wilder fatidical songs. Be a counter-antagonist, break their anti-myths. Where the enemies breed destructions, sow seeds of startling lights. Keep sowing. Time will reap. Weave your songs by whatever means you can. 'What doesn't kill us makes us stronger,' wrote Nietsche. There is no reason why the poet, if possessed of practical intelligence, cannot survive as well as the politician, or the banker. Don't become a dying breed. Dare to stick around for the hard and beautiful harvest. We need you even as we antagonise you. Remember: it is from the strength of your antagonists that you derive your greater authority. They make it absolutely necessary for you to be more than yourself. Follow Melville's precept, which he had nailed to his writing desk: 'Be true to the dreams of thy youth.' After your untimely and much lamented death, we would shout about how much we miss the uniqueness of your voice, your demanding presence, your duende. Don't wait till you're dead to know that in reality the whole of life is on your side.

Poet, be like the tortoise: bear the shell of the world and still manage to sing your transforming dithyrambs woven from our blood, our pain, our loves, our history, our joy. The lonely and inescapable truth simply is that this is the only kingdom you will ever have. This is the home of your song.

CREATIVITY
AND THE MINOTAUR
For Rosemary Clunie

Every true work of art is an enigma. But Picasso's 'Minotauromachy' doubles its power by being an enigma about an enigma. This masterpiece of etching is a pure piece of visual paradox and symbolic prophecy. Executed in the thirties, during the atmosphere of gathering wars, it positively bristles with terror foreshadowed, with darkness already present.

The Minotaur is an old and deep figure in the consciousness of humanity. Out of the depths of our past, it has re-emerged on the stage of history. Half-man, half-bull, it dominates the landscape of this work, blocking out the light, cornering all the other figures. The Minotaur is no longer at the centre of the ancient Cretan labyrinth: it is in the centre of the picture, and the world stage. It has broken out of its lair. The Minotaur is the enigma at the heart of the modern age.

For Camus, the Minotaur is boredom – the boredom

that devours the vitality of the young. For Picasso it is more sinister and complex. The Minotaur's presence makes the world claustrophobic. Its brutish head is inescapable. Roles have been reversed: the Minotaur is striking back. Because we have failed to transform the animal within our labyrinth, the animal within is conquering us, unleashing vengeance.

The awesomeness of the Minotaur is reflected in the frenzied contortion of the horse and the murdered beauty on its back. The bearded man, who should be the defender, is seen fleeing up a ladder. The ladder leads nowhere. His backward-twisted head is the measure of his panic.

Only a little girl faces the Minotaur. She holds a candle aloft in one hand, and proffers flowers with the other. Her serenity is astonishing. The great Minotaur stares at her, sword pointed, but she isn't really looking at him. Her eyes do not judge, her gaze seems to see beyond the horror. She doesn't seem to see the spectre in front of her. She does not see the monster. She is not aware of the danger. Her gaze is gentle. Maybe she doesn't see him as a monster. Maybe she sees him as a big, blind, unloved thing. Maybe the candle is there because she needs light to see by, to offer him flowers. Maybe it's the symbol she offers, the light she shows, which really halts and confounds the enigma.

Might can always be greater than might: and violence

would never have conquered the Minotaur. In a sense, the Minotaur cannot be conquered. It, too, is a part of life, of us, a part of life's duality. The Minotaur, therefore, is not evil. Repellent, sad, a touch pathetic, and fascinating, it is an ambiguous figure. It represents something in us, something that has been ignored, or gone out of control. But when this irrational self bursts out, rampant, what recourse do we have? It is all in the girl, Picasso says, in the purity of heart and motive, in light, and in seeing clearly. This etching is part fairy-tale, asking us to believe in the power of symbols and the gentle triumph of wisdom and love.

> How with this rage shall beauty hold a plea
> Whose action is no stronger than a flower?

With the figure of that little girl Picasso answers Shakespeare's anguished question.

We always need to be reminded of forgotten higher things. True artists are wiser than we think.

NEWTON'S CHILD

Perhaps we should strive towards mythical resonances in our lives. Among many possible images, a human being can be seen as a tree: we should reach out for more light even as we reach deeper into reality for a more solid hold on the earth. We were not born with one eye, with only one thought in our heads, and with only one direction to travel. When we look out on the world with all its multiplicity of astonishing phenomena, do we see that only one philosophy can contain, explain, and absorb everything? I think not. The universe will always be greater than us. Our mind therefore should be like Keats' thoroughfare, through which all thoughts can wander. It should also be a great cunning net that can catch the fishes of possibility.

Maybe our mind should be sensitive to the vastness that lies behind all reality, should be open to the winds and whispers of infinity, and should be able – by inkling and intuition – to enter the hidden realms of the blazing Tyger, the Robin, the Eagle, the Unicorn, and our mysterious humanity. How can we, in the presence of irreducible being, view life from only one perspective – the Cheetah's, the Tyger's or our own? We have the gift of overview, the tower of Imagination. We can place many perspectives side-by-side, we can even inhabit them simultaneously.

In art a complex experiment (if fully realised, and rendered as if natural) is but a sign of and a prayer to the greater glory and sublimity of our secret estate. It is a celebration of our terrestrial intelligence, our spiritual yearning, and the irrepressibility of our mischief and joy.

Better a complex mind behind a seemingly simple thought, than a simple mind behind a seemingly complex thought. The mind should surround what it expresses. Accidental perceptions can sometimes be profound, but it is always best to make the accidental perception into a leavening agent, to extend its radiance and influence throughout the texture of the work. There are few things worse than being exposed by the unabsorbed felicities of chance.

Thoughts solidly crafted like the artefacts of Haphaestus can shape the destiny of generations. Every artist has to be as much a shaper as a diviner. Artists carry their susceptibility to hidden illumination around with them. They go about with half-sight, partially in this world, partially in an invented one, their spine a divining rod, seeking attunement to the source of inspiration. And when a great thought twitches their soul, they have to hide, as if from lightning, and catch the inspiration on the wing, that it may not overwhelm them. Blessed are those who are overwhelmed, and who remember creatively.

Often ideas of great beauty come to us when we are most constrained. You might think there is a kind of perversity to inspiration. There might be. The subconscious loves mischief; its resident forces are trickster deities, Eshu, or Hermes, and other such figures who love tangents, invisibility, boundaries, and enigmas. The subconscious loves games; it is our own internal underworld of combinations, transformations, enchantments, and unfixed shapes.

Creativity, it would appear, should be approached in the spirit of play, of foreplay, of dalliance, doodling, messing around — and then, bit by bit, you somehow get deeper into the matter. But if you go in there with a businessman's solemnity or the fanaticism of some artistic types you are likely to be rewarded with a stiff response, a joyless dribble, strained originality, ideas that come out all strapped up and strangled by too much effort.

★

The creative self has one side facing the dark waters, and the other side facing the bright and joyful firmament. Paradoxically, it flows into all things: and your spirit, in approaching it, should be able to flow into all things, all thoughts, all possible realities. Do not disdain the idle, strange, ordinary, nonsensical, or shocking thoughts which the mind throws up. Hold them. Look at them. Play with them. See where they lead. Every perception or possibility has its own life-span: some have short lives, others keep on growing, and many are open to infusions of greater life.

The artist should never lose the spirit of play. It is curious how sometimes the biggest tasks are best approached tangentially, with a smile in the soul. Much has been written about the seriousness with which important work has to be undertaken. I believe that seriousness and rigour are invaluable, and hard work indispensable – but I want to speak a little for the mysterious and humble might of a playful creative spirit. Playfulness lightens all terrifying endeavours. It humanises them, and brings them within the realm of childhood. The playfulness becomes absorbing, engrossing, all-consuming, serious even. The spirit warms. Memory burns brightly. The fires of intelligence blaze away, and self-consciousness evaporates. Then – wonderfully – the

soul finds the sea; and the usually divided selves function, luminously, as one.

The play soon becomes its own sustenance. 'I wonder
how far I can take this?' the smiling self asks. And the
spirit of the encounter answers by taking leaps into the
unknown, and creating terra firma for itself to land
on. It answers by inventing roads where none exist,
extending ones that do. In short, out of the place
where playfulness and inspiration meet, come ideas and
possibilities more astonishing, more solid, and more
profound than can be pulled out of a solemn and
sententious disposition.

It could well be that the wonders of literature and
the marvels of the creative spirit are the offspring of the
marriage between play and discipline, purpose, and
mastery. An ideal creative genius would be one who
knew how to consciously initiate great play, as well as
how to harness great discipline, towards the most
sublime endeavours.

If nothing else, if that height is beyond us, then at
least a joyful creative attitude to life can transform the
chore and boredom of work into perpetual delight, and
introduce the hint of a blessed smile into the challenges
of our days.

There is a touch of blessedness in the art of writing. It

is sometimes interesting, while writing, to be occupied by the mood you want to render and to let the mood find the words. This assumes a oneness between you and your material, a quality of grace. But the mind often, in the midst of work, functions as its own infallible scanning sensibility, and can almost instantly find the words of the right colour, vibrancy, and tone. It is amazing how much of writing is a combination of mathematics and musical composition, of reason and aesthetics. It is also amazing how much of writing is rewriting; how much is instinctive; how much is simple logic, and the application of so many secret and invisible laws. Take, for example, the law of visuality – the words you actually see on the page. There is, to give another example, the law of the subliminal effect – words that you don't notice but which make you see things more acutely.

Some writing is forceful, ambitious, and immediate; it is all there, it is sensual. Another kind of writing appears simple, does not add up to much on the page, and performs no somersaults. We think one kind of writing is better, but we are sometimes wrong, and sometimes right. When they work both kinds of writing are gifts, and both can be magical.

Some kinds of writing are commonly perceived as the best kind. Some are easier to praise. Some are easier to see. Some are easier to do. And some flatter the reader's intelligence by eliciting clever responses from the clever use of their minds. But too often a lot of writing that impresses us at the time for some reason doesn't go deep into our consciousness. The immediate response to a lot of supposedly good writing is usually more enthusiastic than the response evoked by the memory of it years later. It is sad how much that seemed fine shrinks in time. There is a sad mystery in it.

The best kinds of books, however, have a delightful mystery about them. They inexplicably create powerful feelings, images, moods, worlds, and parallel narratives the farther away in time you are from the reading. They grow in time. They keep re-creating themselves in your consciousness, they keep growing, keep becoming other books, till they become part of your experience, like something lived, or dreamed, or loved, or suffered.

Further encounters with such books make them more. There is no final point of understanding with books that live.

Their effects cannot be aspired to. And writers can never be altogether sure that they have indeed created this rare and living thing. For their mysterious effect can only be felt silently, in the secret chambers of consciousness, in the depths of sleep and forgetfulness, in states of being where the magic of the words can work unseen. This kind of writing keeps living through time, through generations, through stories people tell one another, through our solitudes and moods, and through the ways in which such books make us more creative as we live and change and grow – or even as we face the prospect of dying. These books do not belong to their authors. And so they cannot really take pride in them. They will never truly know the nature of their gifts. That is because these are gifts hurled out into time, hurled out to future friends and affinities. If writers like that are our contemporaries we may never wholly recognise them, or realise what they will come to mean – for we do not inhabit the future; and if we have an inkling of what they are, then we are really waiting for them to die, for only then will the full nature of their splendid gifts begin to give off their eternal and natural light.

The highest kind of writing – which must not be confused with the most ambitious kind – belongs to the realm of grace. Talent is part of it, certainly; a thorough understanding of the secret laws, absolutely. But finding the subject and theme which is in perfect harmony with your deepest nature, your forgotten selves, your hidden dreams, and the full unresonated essence of your life – now that cannot be reached through searching, nor can it be stumbled upon through ambition. That sort of serendipity comes upon you on a lucky day. It may emerge even out of misfortune or defeat. You may happen upon it without realising that this is the work through which your whole life will sing. We should always be ready. We should always be humble. Creativity should always be a form of prayer.

You cannot write well when you have no feelings and no thoughts on the subject. Perhaps when we have to write to order the ill-used creative self, bored with the business of irrelevant and joyless tasks, will simply refuse to come alive when you really need it. You could call this the condition of developing faulty internal relations.

Inspiration is harmony. The mind loves patterns. If you have a creative problem, and you know how to keep your mind open, it usually comes about that the mind thinks of the problem in terms of filling a vacuum, filling a tense space, filling the pattern. One definition of style, or voice, could be: patterns of words guided by self-mastery.

There is no need to panic. The intelligence that shaped the universe shaped you. There is an inner part of us, for ever obscured, for ever mysterious, which is most alive during the process of composition. And that inner part, that inner glow, is timeless, and it functions beyond time. It drinks from deep waters. It has the stillness and the dance and the radiance of the firmament. When one is most absorbed in the act of creation one almost feels that one is wandering in the great corridors of all minds. Creativity makes us part of it all. There is no genuine creative or human problem that cannot be solved if you are serene enough, humble enough, hard-working enough, and if you have learnt the gentle arts of concentration, visualisation, and meditation. For me, tranquillity is the sign of the invisible presence of grace.

There are many mysteries, continents, and planets in writing that we haven't yet discovered. There are many oceans of literary possibilities that we don't suspect exist. We are still like Newton's child, playing on the shore, turning over pebbles, while great possibilities of wonder stretch out ahead of us into eternity. This is the beauty of it all. The full potential of human creativity has not yet been tapped. Along with the ever-renewing miracle of love, this fact is one of the brightest hopes for the human race.

THE JOYS OF
STORYTELLING I

I

It may seem that because we live in a fractured world the art of storytelling is dead. It may seem that because we live in a world without coherent belief, a world that has lost its centre, in which a multitude of contending versions of reality clamour in the mind, that storytelling and enchantment are no longer relevant. This is a sad view. Worse than that, it is a view which implies that we no longer have a basis from which to speak to one another. When we do attempt speech or song we do it sol-ipsistically, in fractured tones. This negative view of storytelling also implies that there are no continuities in the human experience, and no magical places resident in us that we can call up in one another.

The centuries have indeed been brutal. All the great systems have failed, or are failing. The fractured view of history is not even a tragic one, for it has no grandeur. At best it is pathetic, small, ironic, and glancing.

———

It must be remembered, however, that history may be fractured, that certainties have been crumbling, but that the human mystery remains. It is probably just as well that certainties are being broken. Certainty has always been the enemy of art and creativity; more than that it has been the enemy of humanity. In the name of certainties, under its illusory god, people have had an almost medieval belief in the rightness of the violence they have wreaked on others, in the destruction of other people's ways and lives. In the name of certainties, nations and individuals had come to regard themselves as gods. This certainty, whether its name be religion, imperialism, ideology, class, caste, race, or sex, has been the great undoing of our measureless heritage, and has narrowed the vastness of human possibility and marvellous variety.

If the towers of certainty collapse one after another on the great landscape of History and Time, then this represents somewhat wonderfully the triumph of Time over the insane arrogance of human certainties.

Those who suspect that the true beauty of the human dream has not yet emerged from its hidden and silenced places celebrate, albeit with some sadness in their hearts, the fragmentary edifices of certainties strewn about the world. We await without wonder the collapse of the last remaining towers − for then and only then can the beginnings of a true world history and genius flower; only then will a new age of miraculous rivers, hidden dreams, flowers of unsuspected beauty, philosophies of unknown potency emerge and astound future generations; only then might the world hope as one and struggle as one, towards the first universal golden age.

2

On an ocean older than humanity, in a space between old and new, I made a very simple rediscovery. Rolled into a sea-shaped lullaby, aboard a ship bound for America, floating on the dreams of the great ocean god of the Atlantic, with porpoises swimming past under my astonished gaze, I reconnected with something old in me, older than fire, older than rage. I made this discovery accidentally, through one of the serendipities that come upon us when circumventing a fear.

Rocking on the vast expanse of water, I often wandered the corridors of the great ship. And one evening I found myself amongst a crowd who were watching the shimmering conjurations of a magician. I was in the gallery, looking down, and I noticed how the magician circled himself with lights, stage lights, lights of purple and gold and sapphire. He had a piano and on the piano there was a book. He had a wand, hats, white scarves, golden balls, silver ringlets, silk handkerchieves, and all the other brilliant paraphernalia of his trade. But most of all, he had the complete attention of the audience. He had their eyes. He had taken their eyes from them, had divorced them from their senses, lifted them from mid-sea into mid-imagination, mid-fantasy, a country without land, without boundaries, and whose only known laws of gravity are the three laws of enchantment. He had their eyes on his shirt and in his hands, and their ears were in the piano or their ears circled, swirling, in the air, wafted by the languorous strains of invisible music – music suggestive of mystery, voluptuousness, decadence, timelessness, and Prospero: the violin capriccios of Paganini, the *études* of Liszt, the elusive melisma of Chopin. The magician had the hearts of the audience too, and he made them all as one, as one people gazing into an ancient fire, under the awesome mystery of a dark-blue sky, with an emblematic oriental crescent moon above them.

Our ocean-liner magician was suave. He knew that there is nothing people in mid-sea like better than forgetfulness, enchantment, a visual focus, flashes of white, hints of unicorn lights, embodied charisma. He was their magus, their enchanter, dressed in tuxedo, exuding charm and effortless transatlantic professionalism. His props were numerous, his methods both varied and familiar. He titillated the men by having as his assistant a curvaceous blonde woman, partially naked, with hints of perfumed flesh beneath stockings glimmering with little stars.

The magician had a wonderful contraption that saws

people in half, and while he sawed his assistant the collective mouth of the audience gasped and their lost eyes, for a moment, saw blood pouring on the lacquered, polished floor. A woman in the audience cried out, and the magician commanded us all to be silent. When our sights cleared, and the blood vanished, and we were no longer sure if we knew what we were seeing or not, lost as we were in the magician's generation of illusions, he asked a sceptical donnish-looking man to step forward and ascertain if the woman had been cut in half. The don duly did so, and confirmed it; and the woman, wheeled around, indeed showed a remarkable gap in her voluptuous midriff. Then, just as the audience began struggling with their own senses, she was wheeled away, draped with a silk cloth. Then, surrounded by the Mozart of *Don Giovanni*, and with a cry as primeval as any uttered before an ancient fire by a timeless sorcerer making a dead hero manifest to his unbelieving people, and with the gesture of a prophet breaking before our eyes a great tablet of forgotten laws, the transatlantic magician reassembled the fractured woman, and lifted our enchantment into a comfortable realm of applause and reconstituted certainty.

But the magician hadn't finished: before the evening was over he made his wand fly about the room with no cords attached, he sent little stars dancing round him, he turned silk into birds, and made the birds vanish; he pulled money out of a lady's hair (but mysteriously didn't make himself richer); and at the critical moment of the evening he brought down the strange book, and told us the story of a man's pact with the devil (while the lights flickered in mid-ocean) and, while the notes of a Liszt concerto soared, rose, and changed, while the three helpers created confusing sensations by moving across the stage in red gowns and horned masks, and just as the magician, with another odd cry, opened the book – it burst suddenly into flames at the same moment as the auditorium plunged into darkness. No one moved. No one breathed. The audience seemed too astounded at first to applaud. His greatest accomplishment was our silence.

When I went back to my cabin I was mildly exhilarated and unaccountably depressed.

3

In my cabin, looking out over the primordial waters, my mind made journeys back to the time when the sea was still a god, and when fire was a new deity – a deity that brought out terror and storytelling from the hearts of emergent humanity. I seemed then to travel back to those unrecorded ages when communities and families sat huddled beneath the undeciphered sky, gazing into the mystery of fire, with all the terrors of the world lurking about them in the darkness which was also a god. The fire was the home then of the living soul, and the refuge from the unknown shapes and monsters of the growing dark. It was terror that brought out the mystery from which humans gazed into fire, and saw their only hope. It was uncertainty, the unknown, the darkness, and the unquenchable fire in the human breast which made that a time of dread enchantments. And the masters of enchantment, of bringing the dark sky and the howling dark within the realm of the bearable, the masters of keeping terror at bay, were the story-tellers.

The earliest storytellers were magi, seers, bards, griots, shamans. They were, it would seem, old as time, and as terrifying to gaze upon as the mysteries with which they wrestled. They wrestled with the mysteries and transformed them into myths which coded the world and helped the community to live through one more darkness, with eyes wide open, and with hearts set alight.

I can see them now, the old masters. I can see them standing on the other side of the flames, speaking in the voices of lions, or thunder, or monsters, or heroes, heroines, or the earth, or fire itself – for they had to contain all voices within them, had to be all things, and nothing. They had to have the ability to become lightning, to become a future homeland, to be the dreaded guide to the fabled land where the community will settle and fructify. They had to be able to fight in advance all the demons they would encounter, and summon up all the courage needed on the way, to prophesy about all the requisite qualities that would ensure their arrival at the dreamt-of land.

The old masters had to be able to tell stories that would make sleep possible on those inhuman nights, stories that would counter terror with enchantment, or with a greater terror. I can see them, beyond the flames, telling of a hero's battle with a fabulous beast – the beast that is in the hero. I can hear and see them as they raise storms before their people's eyes, make great snakes appear before their mesmerised gaze, as they take them to the deeps of the sea and show them great monster fishes in whose bellies sit the last of human kind in serene acceptance of their fate till they are vomited out near untrodden shores. I can hear their deep voice rising in the dark, imitating the growl of two-headed beasts with resonant names, and I can see that terror-stricken community gather even closer together under the dreadful spell of the ritual stories. The stories were more terrifying than the darkness they feared, or the unknown that they cowered from, or the storms that threatened to tear off the roof of the sky, or their destinies – the greatest terror of them all. The stories, made real to them, and conjured up in their minds by wizened or blind old bards, made all the darknesses more bearable. The community could sleep well that night and carry on the long struggle when dawn, a benign god, brought light for the day's new journeys.

The storyteller's art changed through the ages. From battling dread in words and incantations before their people did in reality, they became repositories of the people's wisdom and follies. They became the living memory of a people. Often, conscripted by kings, they became the memory of a people's origins, and carried with them the long line of ancestries and lineages. Most important of all, they were the living libraries, the keepers of legends and lore. They knew the causes and mutations of things, the herbs, trees, plants, cures for diseases, causes of wars, causes of victory, the ways in which victory often precipitates defeat, or defeat victory, the lineages of gods, the rites humans have to perform to the gods. They knew of follies and restitutions, were advocates of new and old ways of being, were custodians of culture, recorders of change. They kept the oldest and truest dreams and visions of their people alive. They also kept alive the great failings, the healing tragedies of the never-ending journey towards their utopias, the ever-moving dream of happiness.

These old storytellers were the true magicians. They were humanity's truest friends and most reliable guides. Their role was both simple and demanding. They had to go down deep into the seeds of time, into the dreams of their people, into the unconscious, into the uncharted fears, and bring shapes and moods back up into the light. They had to battle with monsters before they told us about them. They had to see clearly. They had to see even what they hadn't seen, and make it more real to us than our most ordinary or most frightening experiences. They lived lives of intense sacrifice, placing their psyches, dreams, hungers, and their lives on the altar of listening, seeing, sensing, confronting. And then they had to render all they had witnessed into comprehendable stories from the other side of the fire, in the deepest of nights.

They risked their sanity and consciousness in the service of dreaming better futures. They risked madness, or being unmoored in the wild realms of unknown interspaces, or being devoured by the unexpected demons of the communal imagination. When great storytellers die, a thousand years of unconfronted journeys, unguided journeys towards the deceptive lights of future civilisations also perish in their silence.

They hid profound truths within innocent-seeming stories. They spoke infuriatingly in riddles. They knew the power and meaning of signs, knew the universe to be a vast system of codes and signs. They compressed eras into enigmas, told secret histories in public ones, and public histories in secret ones. They dwelt in our unconscious, and had to know how to visit the underworld, and return intact. They told of history through stories of the unconscious, and rendered the narratives in our collective and individual dreams – the narratives within our sleep and forgetfulness which are more devastating than the factual narrative of lived history and linear time; internal narratives that are more explosive than facts, and truer.

The old storytellers were the first real explorers and frontierspeople of the abyss. They brought the world within our souls. They made living within and living without as one.

And I think that now, in our age, in the mid-ocean of our days, with certainties collapsing about us, and with no beliefs by which to steer our ways through the dark descending nights ahead – I think that now we need those fictional old bards and fearless storytellers, those seers. We need their magic, their courage, their love, and their fire more than ever before. It is precisely in a fractured, broken age that we need mystery and a reawoken sense of wonder. We need them in order to begin to be whole again. We need to be reminded of the primeval terror again. We need to be humble again. We need to go down to the bottom, to the depths of the heart, and start to live again as we have never lived before. All the terrors are still there. It's we who no longer see them. They are getting ready to pounce on us again. Maybe it has already happened.

4

When I left the magician's performance, as I told you, I was both exhilarated and depressed. In fact, I felt a little twinge of professional envy. The magician had possessed the full attention of the audience. Unlike at most poetry readings, no one had left, not even to ease themselves. His spell was visible in its effect. The magician had so many tools, so many props, so much with which to hold the attention of the audience.

Much later, in my cabin, I read from a verse translation of Homer's *Odyssey*, and fell into a light sleep in which I found myself upon the singing waves, strapped to a mast, struggling to untie myself and jump into the sea to spend my days with the lovely sirens. I had just undone one knot when I found myself in a duel and woke up a moment before Don Quixote's sword pierced me in the ears. It was on waking that I made the simple and obvious rediscovery that I referred to at the beginning of this essay. An obvious discovery, fundamental, but still capable, if fully explored, if flown with into new spaces, of effecting a modest revolution in the practice of one's art. I realised, as you may have guessed, that novelists and wordsmiths have fewer tools than magicians – even magicians of stage and screen – but the tools they have are the most democratic, the most mysterious, and the most deceptive of all. They have the magical absurdity of abstract marks on a blank page, and the imagination of the reader. This is all that is needed. Good words, shaped and steeped in fictionality, and minds to receive them.

The writer, functioning in a magical medium, an abstract medium, does one half of the work, but the reader does the other. The reader's mind becomes the screen, the place, the era. To a large extent, readers create the world from words, they invent the reality they read. Reading, therefore, is a co-production between writer and reader. The simplicity of this tool is astounding. So little, yet out of it whole worlds, eras, characters, continents, people never encountered before, people you wouldn't care to sit next to in a train, planets that don't exist, places you've never visited, enigmatic fates, all come to life in the mind, painted into existence by the reader's creative powers. In this way the creativity of the writer calls up the creativity of the reader. Reading is never passive.

The mystery of storytelling is the miracle of a single living seed which can populate whole acres of human minds. It is the multiplicity of responses which a single text can generate within the mind's unfailing capacity for wonder. Storytellers are a tiny representative of the greater creative forces. And like all artists they should create beauty as best as they can, should serve truth, and remember humility, and when their work is done and finely crafted, arrowed to the deepest points in the reader's heart and mind, they should be silent, leave the stage, and let the imagination of the world give sanctuary.

5

This cannot be said often enough: it is readers who make the book. A book unread is a story unlived. Writers have monumental responsibilities in the execution of their art, but readers also have great responsibilities. They have to make something valuable from their reading. Books are a dialogue between souls. All the untapped energies in great novels should not lie coiled in the pages in vain. All the agony and effort that goes into initiating this dialogue between souls should not be in vain. The reader should bring the best in themselves to meet the best in the writer's work. There could be a greater potential for good in our lives the more one spirit of freedom dances with another. The energies or the serenity within books is meant, finally, to multiply the energies within the reader, or to deepen their serenity. The true destination of books is life, and the living.

The first joy, therefore, is the joy of service. Stories enrich the world. Stories can change lives. They have changed mine. All writers, at some point, have to make this choice, ask this question: what is the purpose of my art? Most, I suspect, if they are inclined to respond at all, might say something like this: 'I have chosen to serve my fellow human beings, to soothe, if I can; to create beauty, if I am lucky; to hint at certain fundamental truths, if I am fortunate; and one way or another to give the best of myself to the world, to people I may never meet, and to do so with the incomplete feeling that it is possibly only on the page, in stories, that we can be so tender to one another, so true, so free, so humane, so brave, and so pure.'

It should be clear by now that it is you, great readers of the world, who are at the root of the storyteller's complex joy.

6

Storytelling is always, quietly, subversive. It is a double-headed axe. You think it faces only one way, but it also faces you. You think it cuts only in one direction, but it also cuts you. You think it applies to others only, when it applies mainly to you. When you think it is harmless, that is when it springs its hidden truths, its uncomfortable truths, on you. It startles your complacency. And when you no longer listen, it lies silently in your brain, waiting. Stories are very patient things. They drift about quietly in your soul. They never shout their most dangerous warnings. They sometimes lend amplification to the promptings of conscience, but their effect is more pervasive. They infect your dreams. They infect your perceptions. They are always successful in their occupation of your spirit. And stories always have mischief in their blood. Stories, as can be seen from my choice of associate images, are living things; and their real life begins when they start to live in you. Then they never stop living, or growing, or mutating, or feeding the groundswell of imagination, sensibility, and character. Stories are subversive because they always come from the other side, and we can never inhabit all sides at once. If we are here, story speaks for there; and vice versa. Their democracy is frightening; their ultimate non-allegiance is sobering. They are the freest inventions of our deepest selves, and they always take wings and soar beyond the place where we can keep them fixed. Stories are subversive because they always remind us of our fallibility. Happy in their serene and constantly-changing place, they regard us always with a subtle smile. There are ways in which stories create themselves, bring themselves into being, for their own inscrutable reasons, one of which is to laugh at humanity's attempt to hide from its own clay. The time will come when we realise that stories choose us to bring them into being for the profound needs of humankind. We do not choose them. Stories may well be some hidden divinity's dialogue with the human soul. The divinity may well be the god of all our hidden and unacknowledged truths. The subversion in storytelling is an important part of the transformation of human beings into higher possibilities.

7

But then, to switch metaphors, storytelling is a house of many mansions, a river with many streams. One thinks of Homer's paradigm of a man who spends twenty years trying to get back home, and who would rather get back to his wife and be mortal than be immortal and dwell with Calypso; or of Ovid, with stories as perpetual metamorphosis, transforming terror into magic; or of Boccaccio, where stories are a way of making the unbearable bearable; or of Scheherezade, with stories as an infinite deferral of death; or of Cervantes, whose Don Quixote preferred to live stories than to read them; or of Aesop, whose stories the people would rather listen to than tolerate the rhetoric of politicians; or the African enchanters, whose stories are rivers reclaiming their own land, and where stories are journeys into the forgotten dreams of the centuries.

8

We all live our lives on this side of the mirror. But when joy touches us, and when bliss flashes inside us briefly, we have a stronger intuition. The best life, and the life we would really want to live, is on the other side of the mirror – the side that faces out to the great light and which hints at an unsuspected paradise.

The greatest stories speak to us with our voice, but they speak to us from the other side.

9

In a fractured age, when cynicism is god, here is a possible heresy: we live by stories, we also live in them. One way or another we are living the stories planted in us early or along the way, or we are also living the stories we planted – knowingly or unknowingly – in ourselves. We live stories that either give our lives meaning or negate it with meaninglessness. If we change the stories we live by, quite possibly we change our lives.

10

Let us extend the heresy. Let's create a little fugue out of it. Our lives are great invisible novels. It makes no difference that they are unwritten or being written.

It has been said that history (and even the universe) is a vast novel, a divine epic, written by God, whose script we cannot decipher.

On a lower level, it has been hinted that we are writing the novels of our lives as we live, and in the living. Sometimes, by dint of foresight, or in a moment of heaven-sent clarity, we manage the great feat of rewriting the novel that our life is becoming, we manage to improve the first draft, we manage to follow an unpromising first chapter with a brilliant second. And sometimes we manage the even greater feat of transforming the unhappy novel of our lives into a happier one – by understanding the bizarre fact that to some extent we are the novelists and composers of our lives. Like the novel, life is an art as well as a craft. While we may not be masters of all the sources of the material and the sublime waters of inspiration, at least we cannot deny the fact that we wield the pen.

11

How many of us try to live with a sense of beauty about the shape of our lives, the same aesthetic sense that novelists and storytellers bring to the shape of their art? And yet there is a hidden message here – the awareness, shared by not a few historical figures, of the links and causes and consequences of our actions, the mathematics of fate; and the sense – ultimately – of living a unique and fascinating destiny.

12

Even when it is tragic, storytelling is always beautiful. It tells us that all fates can be ours. It wraps up our lives with the magic which we only see long afterwards. Storytelling reconnects us to the great sea of human destiny, human suffering, and human transcendence.

13

Storytellers ought not to be too tame. They ought to be wild creatures who function adequately in society. They are best in disguise. If they lose all their wildness, they cannot give us the truest joys.

14

There are two essential joys in storytelling. The joy of the telling, which is to say of the artistic discovery. And the joy of the listening, which is to say of the imaginative identification. Both joys are magical and important. The first involves exploration and suffering and love. The second involves silence and openness and thought. The first is the joy of giving. The second is the joy of receiving. My prayer is to be able to write stories that, to paraphrase T. S. Eliot, can be read so deeply that they are not read at all, but you become the story, while the story lasts. With the greatest writers, you continue to become more of the story long after you have finished it. Of the two joys, the first teaches us humility, while the second deepens our humanity.

THE HUMAN RACE IS

NOT YET FREE

For Salman Rushdie

I

The worst realities of our age are manufactured realities. It is therefore our task, as creative participants in the universe, to redream our world. The fact of possessing imagination means that everything can be redreamed. Each reality can have its alternative possibilities. Human beings are blessed with the necessity of transformation.

2

Writers are the dream mechanisms of the human race. Narrative affects us the ways dreams affect us. They share the same insubstantiality. They both have the hidden capacity to alter reality. Dreams may be freer because they are not composed of words, but when narrative fiction has entered us, it no longer exists as words either.

3

We can control our novels and narratives to some extent, but we cannot control the effect they might have on the world.

And we cannot wholly control our dreams. Sometimes, at night, we dream blasphemous and scandalous things. We dream murders and transformations. We sometimes even dream ourselves into our deepest truths and our unlikely destinies.

4

There is no single way of interpreting dreams that is acceptable to all human beings. Writers create one book which becomes a hundred different books in the minds of those that read it. To some this one book is an object of light, a revelation, an act of liberation. To others, the same book is a monster.

5

Sometimes we dream strange things that make us wonder if there isn't a subversive inner self – an irrepressible and mischievous spirit within – which delights in showing us just how false are the shapes, boundaries and rules by which we lead our lives. This subversive smiling inner self seems intent on showing us that we cannot get away with restricting the freedom and the mysterious nature of human beings.

6

It may be that sometimes our dreams trouble and offend us so much that we want to restrain the impish freedom of this faculty. It may be that this faculty is telling us something that is too truthful for us to take. But this impish faculty of dreaming becomes more insurrective the more we refuse to listen to it.

The things we refuse to face in life feed the enormous appetite of this dangerous truth-telling inner faculty of dreams. The things we refuse to face in life become monsters in our sleep.

7

If the things we face are greater and more important than the things we refuse to face, then at least we have begun the re-evaluation of our world. At least we have started to learn to see and live again.

But if we refuse to face any of our awkward and deepest truths, then sooner or later, we are going to have to become deaf and blind. And then, eventually, we are going to have to silence our dreams, and the dreams of others. In other words, we die. We die in life.

8

When we die in life, it's much easier to watch others dying too; it's much easier to murder the dreams of others, to poison the stream of their lives, to poison their innocence, their love. When we are dead in life we don't notice when little miracles die around us before our deadened gaze.

9

There are many ways to die, and not all of them have to do with extinction. A lot of them have to do with living. Living many lies. Living without asking questions. Living in the cave of your own prejudices. Living the life imposed on you, the dreams and codes of your ancestors.

10

The reality of what we are doing to one another is explosive. The secret content of our lives is terrifying. There is much to scream about. There are great pollulating lies and monsters running around in the seabed of our century. The river within us has become more frozen than ever before. We need much more than Kafka's proverbial axe to crack the ice and make the frozen blood of humanity flow again.

Something is needed to wake us from the frightening depths of our moral sleep.

11

The word 'orthodoxy' conjures up for me a world in which people have reached the final station of how they define themselves.

12

In the silent world, in the shadow world, there are always people dreaming of changing the configuration.

13

There are no longer any stable frontiers between the imagination and the world.

14

The facts of the world are sometimes more imaginative than the productions of our imagination.

15

If reality is also a battle of contending dreams, then our enchantments, our silence, and our highest love should do the fighting.

16

We live inside the dreams of others. We might be imprisoned in them.

17

Exile is a fleeing from one dream to another one. In the process we change, we metamorphose, and our new shapes are never settled.

18

Living is a continual metamorphosis. Everything is change; everything is relative.

19

When we live with overwhelming orthodoxies, the eruptions within are greater. Then our dreams burst the banks of the acceptable.

20

The greater the visible order, the greater the hidden disorder.

21

There can be no absolutes: no absolute good or evil; no absolute way of living. No absolute truth. All truths are mediated and tempered by the fact of living. Being alive qualifies all things.

22

That is perhaps why the ancient Greeks, the Egyptians, the Africans and the Indians have so many gods. Each god is the abstraction of our different attributes and our different selves which need to be acknowledged and nurtured in harmony with the whole. We have to accept our many selves, and our one self. We need to be unified. All our different selves must breathe and be healthy – the side of us that dreams, the part of us that lives beneath the stream of forgetfulness, the body's need for celebration and ecstasy, the soul's need for work, the divine in us that quietly longs for higher union, the erotic in us that craves mortality's immortal joy.

But when any orthodoxy comes along and tries to repress any of these needs or aspects then rebellious dreams are sooner or later going to break out and disturb the good sleep of the land.

23

What hope is there for individual reality or authenticity when the forces of violence and orthodoxy, the earthly powers of guns and bombs and manipulated public opinion make it impossible for us to be authentic and fulfilled human beings?

The only hope is in the creation of alternative values, alternative realities. The only hope is in daring to redream one's place in the world – a beautiful act of imagination, and a sustained act of self-becoming. Which is to say that in some way or another we breach and confound the accepted frontiers of things.

24

The other way is to undertake an integral migration, to become an exile within the interiors of the self. We accept, we change in some way, we go mad. We live two lives, become two people. We dislocate. We implode. Then our secret selves become more real than our external selves.

25

Metamorphosis is the essential condition of a state of affairs. It is the true hidden reality that becomes apparent. The essence of things or people is truer than their visible forms. In a metamorphosis the essential truth overruns the external illusion of truth: as you are, so you become. If you are insensitive to the world you turn into a rhinoceros. But there is more to it than that. The basis of metamorphosis is a simple one. It is anguish, or ecstasy.

26

In a world like ours, where death is increasingly drained of meaning, individual authenticity lies in what we can find that is worth living for. And the only thing worth living for is love. Love for one another. Love for ourselves. Love of our work. Love of our destiny, whatever it may be. Love for our difficulties. Love of life. The love that could free us from the mysterious cycles of

suffering. The love that releases us from our self-impris-
onment, from our bitterness, our greed, our madness-
engendering competitiveness. The love that can make
us breathe again. Love of a great and beautiful cause, a
wonderful vision. A great love for another, or for the
future. The love that reconciles us to ourselves, to
our simple joys, and to our undiscovered repletion. A
creative love. A love touched with the sublime.

27

It isn't Kafka's axes we need. We also need the fires of
love to thaw the frozen streams within. We need to
look at one another afresh, with new eyes. We need to
keep doing that. Every day.

We need to tear down the barriers wisely, or else we
won't be able to get out and nothing will be able to
come in.

28

These are strange times. Many things stifle our dreams.
We may be getting smaller. We should beware of
turning into rhinoceri.

29

We should speak out, cry out, but not too much or we
won't be heard for the monotony of our cry.

We should be silent, and serene, and we should plan,

but we mustn't be too silent; or we won't be heard at all.

30

Before we can create a new world we must first unearth and destroy the myths and realities, the lies and propaganda which have been used to oppress, enslave, incinerate, gas, torture and starve the human beings of this planet.

Facing the lies of history is a basic human responsibility. It is unpleasant to do, but liberating to accomplish. It liberates all of us.

31

All the great religions began as dreams.

32

Religion was the child of suffering and compassion. Suffering is the farthest condition from divinity, but see how all the great religions embrace it. In their purest state, before they busied themselves with the legislation of our lives, and enforced these legislations with earthly powers alien to the immanent source, the great religions brought the infinite compassion of the divine closer to humanity.

33

If anyone questions the validity of these great religions, it may be because they have failed us, let us down, made us smaller. By 'us' I do not mean adherents and the devout. I mean the entire human race. For in their names, in their codes and earthly domination, they have unleashed nightmares upon us. They have unleashed pogroms, beastly wars, vile inquisitions; they have sanctified slavery, racial hatred, and an almost universal uncharitability.

34

It may be that in the dream of their orthodoxy some of the great religions lost touch with noble love that inspired and sustained their births in the first place. They lost touch with the suffering of the people, with hunger. They lost touch with the basic compassion without which even the most beautifully inspired religion becomes an empty shell of dogma.

35

It may be that writers too have failed us. For, seduced by their freedom, their freedom to entertain, they may have been ignoring the monsters growling in our sleep, monsters that may, one day, devour us.

36

Writers have one great responsibility: to write beautifully, which is to say to write well. Within this responsibility is that of being truthful. To charm, to amuse, to enchant, to take us out of ourselves, these are all part of beauty. But there is a parallel responsibility: and that is to sing a little about the realities of the age, to leave some sort of magical record of what they saw and dreamt while they were alive (because they can't really do it the same way when dead), and to bear witness in their unique manner to the beauties, the ordinariness, and the horrors of their times.

37

Writers are dangerous when they tell the truth.

38

Writers are also dangerous when they tell lies.

39

We are all witnesses.

40

Carry on for as long as life carries you.

___

41

If you can't give, you may as well learn.

42

Sometimes the opposite is best.

43

It is not what you have experienced that makes you greater, but what you have faced, what you have transcended, what you have unlearned.

44

The best things are beyond words.

45

The human race is not yet free.

THE JOYS OF
STORYTELLING II

I

When I write of storytelling I use the word 'joys' with a certain touch of irony. I know as well as anyone else how dangerous stories are, and how dangerous for the storyteller they can be. Colleagues have been jailed, tortured, murdered, poisoned, brutalised, hounded into exile, excommunicated, excoriated, and driven mad because of the joys of storytelling. Colleagues have died homeless, in the streets, unloved, unread, misunderstood, shunned, thought mad, ostracised, and have driven themselves into the dark spaces of the imagination from which there is no return, in pursuit of the joys of storytelling.

Art is a harsh goddess: her gifts are ambiguous. On her altars, many have perished. I can think of one, already an icon of free-speech, who is a visible prisoner of our age, under a death sentence, a death-in-waiting, because of the ironic joys.

Storytelling, practised with full consciousness and an

oxygenated sense of responsibility, is one of the most dangerous and liberating of human activities. Life is dangerous. It is not surprising that stories are also sometimes dangerous. A mutant star, red hot in its brief ascendancy, sometimes rules over the fates of true storytellers. But another star, golden in its universal glow, confers great hidden benedictions and blessings on practitioners and readers alike.

Regardless of the ambiguous dark side, artists always feel the craftsman's cool ecstasy and the dreamer's serene joy when creating. And the reader always feels the joy in the dangers when immersing.

2

In storytelling there is always transgression, and in all art. Without transgression, without the red boundary, there is no danger, no risk, no *frisson*, no experiment, no discovery, and no creativity. Without extending some hidden or visible frontier of the possible, without disturbing something of the incomplete order of things, there is no challenge, and no pleasure, and certainly no joy. All true artists suspect that if the world really knew what they were doing they would be punished. Quietly, or dramatically, storytellers are reorganisers of accepted reality, dreamers of alternative histories, disturbers of deceitful sleep.

The transgression may appear to be perfectly innocent and blameless, and even singularly undramatic. It could take the form of simply entering the inner life of another, or being old-fashioned in an era that favours restless experiment, or in favouring narrative in a time that prefers fractured voices. More quixotically, it could take the form of going boldly and brightly against the accepted canons of the age.

The transgression could take a more extreme form – that of saying something so true that it is shocking. There is nothing more shocking or more dangerous or more upsetting to individuals and nations than truth. Giving truth direct narrative expression is to give it a public explosion. The truth – Truth – SHRIEKS: it wakes up all the hidden bullies, the hidden policemen, and the incipient dictators and tyrants of the land. The truth could simply be something that everyone sees and knows already, something that we all live with, sleep with, and wake up to, and die as a result of – the truth could be something so obvious and familiar, but which no one has uttered. It could be there, alive, dormant, visible to all like a white mountain, like an ugly song, like a bleeding face, but no one has uttered its existence, no one has spoken its reality, no one has really seen it, burned in it, agonised in its suppuration, and finally cried it out. And while it lives, uncried out, it devours us, this unacceptable truth that we accept in silence.

The truth can be our hidden selves turned monstrous (and visible to us in the mirror if only we look with the good eye and not the askew eye); or the truth could be the pollulating bacteria of our secret desires (agendas), and all the unrealities and lies and all the consequences of our strange unhappy actions that we spend all our time hiding from and avoiding. Praise be unto those that cry out the truth; for they are cultural and spiritual heroes.

Transgression can also simply reside in creating a beautiful thing. Sometimes the creation of a beautiful thing in a broken resentful age can be an affront to the living, a denial of their suffering. Sometimes beauty can be accusatory. It can place an intolerable question mark over the most complacent and thick-skinned lives. Beauty can become a burden, an unbearable exposure of collective cowardice and sloth and smallness of spirit in an era of malice, an era of failure.

The joy of transgressing beautifully, of taking readers to places they wouldn't willingly go, this joy of seducing or dragging readers in spite of themselves to places deep in them where wonders lurk beside terrors, this delicate art of planting delayed repeat explosions and revelations in the reader's mind, and doing this while enchanting them – this is one of the most mysterious joys of all. It suggests that, at bottom, and never wanting to admit it, we really want to face the hidden Minotaur within, we

65

want the drains unblocked within, we want the frozen river of our blood and compassion to flow again, we want the pain so that we can be free. It is just that we want this unpleasant job of facing the dead and rotting thoughts, habits, desires, notions, and traditions to be done with our collusion, with our secret consent. And we would much prefer to be enchanted or to laugh or to be taken out of ourselves while the horrors are being faced, while the ghosts are being exorcised. And we hope afterwards that we will be lighter for it all, and that the gods of harmony will again, for a while, reside in us. With great books we are sometimes granted this grace.

3

There are no joys without mountains having been climbed. There are no joys without the nightmares which precede them and spring them into the light.

I have hinted at some of the joys of storytelling, now let me rhapsodise briefly about the nightmares of the art.

There is the unnatural possession by an idea, the insomnia of writing, the intractability of the material, the impossibility of fully realising all the subtle possibilities of one's heaven-sent ideas or one's hell-sent notions. There is the pain and suffering of life, and then the agony that is part of the work, and which also informs it. There is the horror of never being able to write again, the misunderstanding of the work, the too quick understanding of critics and friends, the loneliness and solitude of writing, the difficult responsibility of speaking out, and the necessity of silence. There is the great suffering that is an intrinsic part of love, the love of one's work, the love of the world, and of humanity. There is the unbargained-for cost of telling stories – the hounding by dictators, military leaders, spy networks, secret services, all those with their own agendas, all those who like or dislike only through the screen or filter of their ideologies or insecurities. There are other costs – the death-threats, the enmities incurred by the innocence of the word, the demons of rivalry, the degrading competition which leads the best practitioners, if they submit, away from their beautiful journey. The more frightening nightmares lie in the hidden menace of writing, the possible boundaries of art which shade off into the mists of madness, the possibility that the writer can get unmoored in the imagination, lost in the ocean of the unconscious, lost in the dark realms of the mind, an explorer who never returns from the arctic wastes and mountains of the interior. And then there is the silence of the world, an indifference in which the work has to find its way, finding fellow spirits and friends, or creating its own earth of affection from which to grow and flower.

4

The joys that spring from the challenges are profound. And the challenges are always there. As long as there are human beings there will be challenges. Let no one speak to me of frontiers exhausted, all challenges met, all problems resolved. There is always the joy of discovering, uncovering, and forging new forms, new ways, new structures of enchantment, new narratives, new kinds of storytelling, of slipping into the reader's mind, of fascinating, of stimulating and disturbing the world's certainties and asking strong new questions, or finding new solutions to ancient conundrums of narrative and reality.

There is always the joy of rediscovering old ways of telling stories, of stumbling upon paths and roads not fully travelled along, of extending old lodes, old pleasures, of continuing old dreams.

There is always the joy of finding new ways of telling stories without telling stories, new ways of sustaining interest, of making the reader turn the page, new ways of lodging hidden or unstated narratives in the mind – compacted narratives, tangential fictions which are in fact whole long periods of folded time.

There is the joy of creating glinting images, submarine lights, wonderful philosophies, and narratives which are melodies, melodies which are moods, moods which will become tracts of childhood and forgotten lovely moments. To create stories and moods which retroactively become a living dreaming part of the reader's experience, to awaken dormant enchantments, to face concealed terrors, to uncover fears and survive them in stories, to do these things in the reader's colluding mind, seems to me to belong to the small unsung miracles of the narrative art.

We are living in an age of discovery and exploration. There are new frontiers in science, astronomy, mathematics, molecular biology, and communications. It is no surprise that there should also be new frontiers being explored in art. This is especially true in visual art with all its new chaotic outgrowths in this long transitional era when many things are being born and their newness still shocks and repels us. If the artists continue to develop, in retrospect this may be seen as an era of immense experimentation and energy, of the extension of old boundaries, the exploration of unexhausted mines and quarries. In literature, this pushing back of the frontiers lies in the marvel of planting beautiful epiphanic dynamites within innocent-seeming texts or in obscure-seeming books. This feeling that books, that words can once again trouble the sleep of ancient powers; this joyful challenge to the centrality of realism; this eternal questioning of what reality really is; this healing assault on homogeneity; this quest for magical new realms; this playful ambush on the ivory tower and its guardsmen who police the accepted frontiers of what is considered valid in narrative terms; this unsung age of happy and tragic literary warriors and enchanters and healers; this creation of texts which are dreams that keep changing, fluid texts which rewrite themselves when the reader isn't looking, texts which are dreams that change you as you read them, dreams which are texts which you write in the duration of contact between the eye and the page; all these marvels, acts of private and public courage, all this and much more constitutes for me the joys of storytelling. In the struggle to extend our song, we are all of us extending and participating in the ever unfolding story of humanity and literary tradition – but extending it, I hope, not only on to musty shelves where well-meaning scholars make smaller the worlds within words, but extending it, I pray, into the raw world, into the dreams of the living, into their struggles, their suffering, their joys.

LEAPING OUT OF

SHAKESPEARE'S TERROR

Five Meditations on Othello

I

I haven't been able to stop thinking about *Othello* since I saw a production of the play in London's Barbican. It was the first time I had seen it performed on stage. As far as I could tell, I was the only black person in the audience. The seats beside me were occupied by three white girls. They noisily crackled their packets of sweets and giggled a lot. I wanted to tell them to be quiet. But I suspected that if I spoke faces would turn towards me. After a while I couldn't bear it any longer. When I spoke, what I feared happened. Faces turned, eyes lit up in recognition. My skin glowed. I felt myself illuminated, unable to hide.

I used to agree with C. L. R. James that *Othello* is not a play about race. The Royal Shakespeare Company thought so as well. They had Ben Kingsley play Othello in the tradition of the Arab Moor that Edmund Kean made popular in the nineteenth century. Ben Kingsley played the part lyrically, it was obvious that he had been doing some unsuccessful weight-lifting to give the character the stature it deserves, but there were times when his colour made nonsense of the role. The stage lighting often made it difficult to see the difference between his complexion and that of the other actors and actresses. The chromatic tension of the play was thereby rendered harmless. In addition, they imposed on the play a vaguely homosexual theme and a psychiatric condition, the Othello syndrome, a form of psychotic jealousy. None of these helped to make the play credible. These three elements join the long theatrical tradition of evading the terrors that are at the heart of the play.

Often, when people don't really want to face something, they become pretentious. The whole business of Othello as an Arab was popularised by Samuel Coleridge and Charles Lamb. They did not want to face the full implications of Othello's blackness. They did not want him in their dreams. They also did not want to confront the powerful sexual element in the play. If you take away Othello's colour then you don't really have the magnitude of the tragedy. A 'tawny Othello' is much more comfortable to take. If it did not begin as a play about race, then its history has made it one.

The emotional explosiveness of *Othello* depends

utterly on seeing it on stage. Othello's colour is not real on the page. It can be avoided. Coleridge confessed to the 'beautiful compromise' he made in reading the play. But when he saw it on stage he was revolted by the 'wedded caresses' of Othello and Desdemona. Reducing the colour diminishes the force of the sex. Together they can be quite unbearable.

Shakespeare chose his tragic figure well, and then stacked the cards against him. Othello is the only black man in the universe of the play. He is isolated by colour. He cannot hide. And his position of great authority in society makes his isolation deeper. It is a terrifying position to be in. Honourable, trusting, and surrounded by people who might see him as their worst nightmare. The loneliness of colour made worse by the solitude of power. Trapped in a code of honour, to whom could he turn? Who could he trust? It was safer for him to trust those who seemed trustworthy. To begin to doubt would bring on insanity, for he would have to doubt everyone. And then his mortal terror would begin. He would find himself in the labyrinths of that nightmare of history from which there is no escape. That is perhaps why towards the end of the play his dementia thunders as if in the monstrous echo chamber of his own skin.

2

Every age presents *Othello* in relation to how they perceive *the other*. What else can explain the residual hostility of critics towards black actors playing the role? It took thirty-two years for English critics to accept Ira Aldridge in the nineteenth century. His Othello was successful everywhere else. When the celebrated Paul Robeson played the part in 1943 critics said it was like seeing the play for the first time and that Iago became 'a credible villain' when a black man acted Othello. And yet, Othello, fifty years later, continues to be white underneath.

Our perception of the other gives the measure of our humanity, our courage, and our imagination. Iago represents those who cannot accept the other. He cannot accept himself. He makes colour the victim of his failings. The imagery of black as unnatural comes from Iago. He smears it through the play. It is an extraordinary idea: Shakespeare presents this character who is black, and therefore visually alien, and then shows that he is not so alien after all, and paints his humanity right down to his jealous soul. On the other hand we have Iago, who is white, familiar, but who is actually the real alien to humanity and love. It's almost as if Shakespeare was saying: 'It is not those who look different who are the real strangers. For the dangerous ones to succeed in their evil they will be of your familiar colour, and speak with your voice. Don't look for them in startling differences. Look for them within, where they are harder to find.' Iago is a schemer who functions, unrecognised, in the pack, in the crowds.

Iago is a lonely and bitter man. He is the man who utterly refuses to transcend himself. He does not accept reality and he refuses to face history. And yet he is in his twisted way an intelligent man. He has not found the vocation in which to utilise his considerable imaginative gifts. He is so seemingly friendly, so seemingly on your side, he is all appearance. He is the supreme test for those who will not see clearly; who will not see deeply into people. He thinks more intensely than anyone else in the play. In fact, he has the mind of a playwright, manipulating people around his plots. When the plot gets out of hand, when the characters don't behave as expected, like a poor playwright he kills them off. Iago is the scourge of those whose thinking is muddled. He depends on their faulty vision to pervert reality.

One of the great themes of the play, for me, is the war between Appearance and Reality. Appearance strives to be, but Reality is. Appearance can command the gaze, distort things, but Reality is the eternal present. It is what things are in all their secret phases. It is what Appearance strives to become. Reality is the future of all secrets.

Othello is caught in the nightmare that history has

made real. And there is something frightening about a majestic man who believes what they say about him. He believes too much in appearances. Here is a man of royal birth, who was taken as a slave, and rose to become a general. Whatever bitterness or bewilderment he might have had has been taken from him. In their place he has been fed bubbles of power. He fed them to himself.

Iago is the most perceptive person in the play: so coldly does he calculate the shallowness of Othello's rise, how much he must have paid, how much rage he must repress. And because Othello can't really release his rage, as it would hinder his rise, he can't transform his anger into something higher. He can't therefore transcend his jealousy when it swoops into his soul like a green bird of prey. All Iago has to do is get that repressed rage to turn on itself and to open up in Othello the element of self-destruction.

Othello can't really be honest to himself. He couldn't have risen that high and in such fearful isolation if he were. Unlike Iago, he accepts too much. He even wholly accepts the blind logic of the world in which he has sacrificed his history for ambition. That is why he has to be so trusting. Trapped in ambition, marked by his colour, refusing to confront his predicament, he is the authentic self-betrayer. He is the white man's myth of the black man. But he is also a negative myth for black people in the West. Signposts along roads that can lead to hell also have their own peculiar value.

3

It must be admitted that there is something unbelievably simple about Othello. He comfortably personifies jealousy, and his particular manifestation of it is taken as a quality of his otherness. But there he is, a man of royal birth, taken as a slave, and he has no bitterness. He doesn't possess an ounce of anger, or even a sense of injustice. It is difficult to believe that he has got so far as a warrior, climbed so high in office, and yet possesses no cunning and no ability to penetrate appearances. The most irritating thing of all is his nobility, which, in his predicament, is a sort of naïvety. When a black man is portrayed as noble in the West it usually means that he is neutralised. When white people speak so highly of a black man's nobility they are usually referring to his impotence. It is Othello's neutrality and social impotence that troubles me.

James Baldwin has said that people will face in your life only what they would face in theirs. But to this must first be added the condition that people accept your humanity as essentially equal to theirs. Shakespeare, as a white man of his era, could not fully concede Othello an equal status of humanity. It seems that the only way white people can see black people, and begin to accept them, without really having to face them, is by lessening their internal realities. Their external difference, their skin colour, is romanticised, taken as exotic.

And their souls are filled with blankness. This is why a lot of white people can know what black people suffer daily all over the globe and not be really bruised in their humanity: because they assume that black people are used to their pain, that they feel things differently, and that suffering is their unchanging condition. When you reduce the reality of the other there is the obvious benefit of not having to face the fullness of their being, their contradictions, their agonies.

Those who hate black people and those who romanticise them mean the same thing when one speaks of the colour as ugly and the other speaks of it as attractive. Both of them deny black its own unique condition and existence unto itself. The weirdest thing about Othello is that his colour is empty of history. It is the accepted thing to comment on Othello's jealousy, but few critics seem to realise that his colour, his otherness, must imply a specific history in white society. It seems that into the vessel of Othello's skin, Shakespeare poured whiteness. It is possible that Othello actually is a blackened white man.

He certainly is a lost man. His author cheats him of a satisfying period of sex with Desdemona. Instead of sex, Othello is allowed coitus interruptus. Instead of anger, he is given an almost idiotic naïvety. He has no real friends. In spite of his apparel of power and glory, he is a naked man, a deluded man. And why does he have to be trapped in that unending cycle of murder and suicide? Does the denial of someone's humanity inexorably lead them to murder? Or is it that in an abnormal situation only an abnormal action becomes possible? And when no human solution seems possible is suicide the inevitable consequence? Or is suicide a twisted affirmation of freedom? It is also a fantasy, a wishing away of reality: it avoids the problem of race. It is amazing that Othello's suicide is seen as an extension of his nobility, when in fact it is the inescapable logic of his impotence. The whole machinery of the play is set in motion by the presence of this lone black man. By the end he has killed himself. Iago who is responsible for so many deaths is dragged away, unrepentant. Without Othello, the universe of the play becomes homogenous, diminished. There are always alternatives. We always need the other.

4

In three centuries of Othello committing murder and suicide on the stage no significant change in attitude towards black people has occurred. I doubt that *Othello* really disturbs people as much as it should. Society has become smothered by complacency. Add to this the fact that Othello as a lone black man on the stage is not threatening. White audiences must merely look upon his phenomenon. It is a basic truth of literature that if you can't enter the centre of a work, then it can't really shake you. How can white people imagine themselves in Othello's skin? History does not support it. Othello is a character with only one road leading out of him, but none lead into him. The black person's response to Othello is more secret, and much more anguished, than can be imagined. It makes you unbearably lonely to know that you can empathise with them, but they will rarely empathise with you. It hurts to watch Othello.

Which brings me to another element. Othello is powerless, and Iago the real enemy, and yet I can't wholly blame Othello for trusting him. Of all the people in the play, with the natural exception of Desdemona, Iago is the only one who expresses what he feels for Othello. He is lying, but nonetheless he expresses. It means a lot to the isolated to have someone declare their affection. It means a lot to be loved.

Any black man who has gone out with a white woman knows that there are a lot of Iagos around. If the woman is desirable then the situation is more insidious. The question the new Iagos ask themselves is: why him and not me? Then they might put it down to the myth of the black man's sexuality – a myth invented by white people in the first place. Iago's obsession depends obviously on Othello's success. If Othello were a failure and hadn't won Desdemona's love he would not have begun to exist in Iago's hell. It is also crucial that Iago is a failed human being. He is full of self-loathing. The real jealousy at work in the play is not Othello's, but Iago's. When he speaks of jealousy as a green-eyed monster Iago knows what he is talking about. He's been there. He's stuck there. He has lived with jealousy for a long time. The fascinating and at the same time repellent thing about Iago is his refusal to confront his failure. The angle of his humanity is very thin. He is the man of short cuts. And so he becomes a specialist in the art of projecting his bitterness. And to crown all this: he has to mask his failure, mask his resentment, his self-obsession. And so he mingles with the crowd.

Iago today would not be a member of a fanatical racist group. He is not *that much* of a failure. He would attend the right marches, say the right things, and he would be unmistakably *vocal* in his objection to racism. He would be invisible because he is – almost – like everyone else. He lives in the closed universe between cynicism and hell. He is the perfect hypocrite in the sense that you would never think of applying the word to him. And he is an almost flawless actor and a superb ironist. Most of what Iago says has a sinister truth. It is the fact that he speaks from his own condition which gives his utterances their weird and elusive honesty. His smile should send shudders of terror through us. But it warms us a little, because we despise him and feel bad about it, because he too is human, and more seriously because we don't really know him. But he knows us. He has insinuated himself into our lives. And he loathes us, loathes everything. And in our midst he spins his web of hate. Iago is a more authentic creation than Othello. Wherever human beings fail to transcend aspects of themselves there lie the conditions for the birth of an Iago. He is the universal negative man, foil for heroes. There isn't one of us who hasn't glimpsed that curiously satisfying vengeance of drawing the hated world into the depths of our own hell. It is Iago's complete and secretive dedication which makes him so unique.

Othello, today, would not be a radical. He is too ambitious to let anger get in the way. He has come from nothing and has fought his way up in a new world. He wouldn't want to face the truth about himself because it would destroy him. He wouldn't want to face the falsity of his yearnings. To face his predicament would mean accepting the fact that he has become a willing victim of the dream that enslaved him in the first place. He is merely rising up the ladder available to him, not building his own.

And then there is Desdemona, innocent and sweet and passive. She and Othello are an unfortunate pair. Neither of them has any guile. She is too young to perceive the danger Othello is in. She takes too much for granted and believes too much in the simplicity of everything and everyone. They are mutually deluded. What did she see in him? She saw his nobility, rather than his vulnerability, his strength, rather than the weakness of his position. She is just the type who likes romances and is seduced by exoticism. Today she might be an ardent lover of a glamorised Africa. She would be just the kind of girl who believes that love makes everything right, and that the world would want for her what she wants for herself. She would have heard of slavery but never have thought about it. She would be shocked to hear that black people are treated badly because of their colour, that they have their homes burnt down, and are beaten up and mercilessly discriminated against. She would be shocked because she has never been allowed to confront reality, to face the Medusa-like truths of the world. The source of her delusion is ignorance. She is the redemption and the victim of her history.

5

Desdemona fell in love with Othello because of his stories. He had lived a heroic life. Her father thought

Othello had used sorcery on her. There is no greater sorcery than poetry, than the imagination of the story-teller. Desdemona is a bit of a rebel and her humanity is large. But humanity without scepticism, without knowledge, is dangerous. In real terms she would not find happiness in her choice unless she became a little wise along the way, and the costliest price is always paid for wisdom: the tearing down of as many illusions and lies as the human frame can bear. She would have to love Othello without illusions. It would be a hard kind of love, a rigorous love, that demands constant vigilance. She would have to alter the way she sees her history, and that would alter almost everything else. She would have to be strong. There would be many compensations but she would have to manage the difficulty of being both romantic and wise. And this is the crux of Desdemona's situation. The romantic reduces black people to a fantasy. And then they love the illusion they themselves have created. They do not face black people as they are, each in their own particular individuality. Othello and Desdemona are a doomed alliance: for he doesn't face her reality either. He never questions the true basis of her love, and consequently doesn't understand her illusions, her lack of cunning and fear. Neither of them knew their predicament and so they didn't stand a chance. And love alone is never enough. That is how those who remain unaware, blind to their predicament, are always betrayed. They are betrayed as much by those who don't care about them as by those who love them.

I think that the play is less about jealousy than about accepting the other, about opening the doors of consciousness to more of reality. Or having to become less. Rejecting is easy: all it takes is confusion and ignorance. But facing the complexity of others, their history, their raw humanity – that takes courage, and is rare.

Whose heart is not pierced when at the end of the play Othello asks Ludovico that in his letters telling of the tragedy he should 'speak of me as I am: nothing extenuate, Nor set down in malice. Then you must speak of one that loved not wisely, but too well'? These are the crucial lines of the play. Speak of me as I am. Don't beautify me. Don't simplify me. Don't make me less. Don't make me more either. I am not sure if Shakespeare faced up to that injunction, which is probably the most challenging to a writer. But he put the injunction there. And in doing so he spoke from the depths of Othello's life. That failure to love wisely applies to every main figure in the play – to Desdemona, to her father, to Iago – and to all of us. Here Othello is speaking at the threshold of death. An incomplete creation, a man who throws no shadows, a man who has no secret life, he is about to pass into our dreams. It doesn't really matter that Shakespeare didn't, and quite possibly couldn't, get Othello fully in focus, nor looked at him closely enough. What matters is that because of Shakespeare's genius Othello haunts the English stage. He won't go away. He is always there on the stage, a reminder of his unexplained presence in the white consciousness, and a symbol of the fact that black people and white are bound on the terrible bed of history. Doomed to his relentless cycle, he will not vanish from our dreams. And yet I dream of ways of liberating him from that bondage.

A friend of mine insists that you can choose your sins. You can also choose your nightmares. Somewhere between marriage and murder Othello must wake up to the necessity of vigilance. Leaping out of Shakespeare's terror, he could stand transcendent. Franz Fanon might have been thinking of the long nightmare at the end of Othello's sleep when he wrote in the closing sentences of *Black Masks, White Skins*: 'O my body, make of me a man who always questions.'

When victims stop seeing themselves as victims and discover the power of transformation, forces are born on this planet. The possibilities of a new history depend on it. What is done with these possibilities depends on how wisely we love. And ultimately we are bound in fate with whoever the other may be. We are bound in the fact that we have to deal with one another. There's no way round it. Rilke seemed to be saying something of this when he wrote: 'That's what fate means:/ to be facing each other/ and nothing but each other/ and to be doing it for ever.'

The way we see the other is connected to the way we see ourselves. The other is ourselves as the stranger.

BEYOND WORDS

For Robert Fraser

I

We began before words, and we will end beyond them.

It sometimes seems to me that our days are poisoned with too many words. Words said and not meant. Words said *and* meant. Words divorced from feeling. Wounding words. Words that conceal. Words that reduce. Dead words.

If only words were a kind of fluid that collects in the ears, if only they turned into the visible chemical equivalent of their true value, an acid, or something curative – then we might be more careful. Words do collect in us anyway. They collect in the blood, in the soul, and either transform or poison people's lives. Bitter or thoughtless words poured into the ears of the young have blighted many lives in advance. We all know people whose unhappy lives twist on a set of words uttered to them on a certain unforgotten day at school, in childhood, or at university.

We seem to think that words aren't things. A bump on the head may pass away, but a cutting remark grows with the mind. But then it is possible that we know all too well the awesome power of words – which is why we use them with such deadly and accurate cruelty.

We are all wounded inside in some way or other. We all carry unhappiness within us for some reason or other. Which is why we need a little gentleness and healing from one another. Healing in words, and healing beyond words. Like gestures. Warm gestures. Like friendship, which will always be a mystery. Like a smile, which someone described as the shortest distance between two people.

Yes, the highest things are beyond words.

That is probably why all art aspires to the condition of wordlessness. When literature works on you, it does so in silence, in your dreams, in your wordless moments. Good words enter you and become moods, become the quiet fabric of your being. Like music, like painting, literature too wants to transcend its primary condition and become something higher. Art wants to move into silence, into the emotional and spiritual conditions of the world. Statues become melodies, melodies become yearnings, yearnings become actions.

When things fall into words they usually descend. Words have an earthly gravity. But the best things in us are those that escape the gravity of our deaths. Art wants to pass into life, to lift it; art wants to enchant, to transform, to make life more meaningful or bearable in its own small and mysterious way. The greatest art was probably born from a profound and terrible silence — a silence out of which the deepest enigmas of our lives cry: why are we here? What is the point of it all? How can we know peace and live in joy? Why be born in order to die? Why this difficult one-way journey between the two mysteries?

Out of the wonder and agony of being come these cries and questions and the endless stream of words with which to order human life and quieten the human heart in the midst of our living and our distress.

The ages have been inundated with vast oceans of words. We have been virtually drowned in them. Words pour at us from every angle or corner. They have not brought understanding, or peace, or healing, or a sense of self-mastery, nor has the ocean of words given us the feeling that, at least in terms of tranquillity, the human spirit is getting better.

At best our cry for meaning, for serenity, is answered by a greater silence, the silence that makes us seek higher reconciliation.

I think we need more of the wordless in our lives. We need more stillness, more of a sense of wonder, a feeling for the mystery of life. We need more love, more silence, more deep listening, more deep giving.

2

When the angels of the Bible spoke to human beings, did they speak in words? I don't think so. I think the angels said nothing, but they were heard in the purest silence of the human spirit, and were understood beyond words.

On a more human scale there are many things beyond.

A mother watches her child leave home. Her heart is still. Her eyes are full of tears and prayer. That is beyond.

An old man with wrinkled hands is carrying his grandchild. With startled eyes the baby regards his grandfather. The old man, with the knowledge of Time's sadness in his heart, and with love in his eyes, looks down at the child. The meeting of their eyes. That is beyond.

A famous writer, feeling his life coming to an end, writes these words: 'My soul looks back and wonders how I got over.'

A young woman, standing on a shore, looks out into an immense azure sea rimmed with the silver line of the horizon. She looks out into the obscure heart of destiny, and is overwhelmed by a feeling both dark and oddly joyful. She may be thinking something like this: 'My soul looks forward and wonders – just how am I going to get across.' That is beyond.

3

A flamenco dancer, lurking under a shadow, prepares for the terror of her dance. Somebody has wounded her in words, alluding to the fact that she has no fire, or *duende*. She knows she has to dance her way past her limitations, and that this may destroy her for ever. She has to fail, or she has to die. I want to dwell for a little while on this dancer because, though a very secular example, she speaks very well for the power of human transcendence. I want you to imagine this frail woman. I want you to see her in deep shadow, and fear. When the music starts she begins her dance, with ritual slowness. Then she stamps out the dampness from her soul. Then she stamps fire into her loins. She takes on a strange enchanted glow. With a dark tragic rage, shouting, she hurls her hungers, her doubts, her terrors, and her secular prayer for more light into the spaces around her. All fire and fate, she spins her enigma around us, and pulls us into the awesome risk of her dance.

She is taking herself apart before our sceptical gaze.

She is disintegrating, shouting and stamping and dissolving the boundaries of her body. Soon she becomes a wild unknown force, glowing in her death, dancing from her wound, dying in her dance.

And when she stops – strangely gigantic in her new fiery stature – she is like one who has survived the most dangerous journey of all. I can see her now as she stands shining in celebration of her own death. In the silence that follows, no one moves. The fact is that she has destroyed us all.

Why do I dwell on this dancer? I dwell on her because she represents for me the courage to go beyond ourselves. While she danced she became the dream of the freest and most creative people we had always wanted to be, in whatever it is we do. She was the sea we never ran away to, the spirit of wordless self-overcoming we never quite embrace. She destroyed us because we knew in our hearts that rarely do we rise to the higher challenges in our lives, or our work, or our humanity. She destroyed us because rarely do we love our tasks and our lives enough to die and thus be reborn into the divine gift of our hidden genius. We seldom try for that beautiful greatness brooding in the mystery of our blood.

You can say in her own way, and in that moment, that she too was a dancer to God.

That spirit of the leap into the unknown, that joyful giving of the self's powers, that wisdom of going beyond in order to arrive here – that too is beyond words.

All art is a prayer for spiritual strength. If we could be pure dancers in spirit we would never be afraid to love, and we would love with strength and wisdom. We would not be afraid of speech, and we would be serene with silence. We would learn to live beyond words, among the highest things. We wouldn't need words. Our smile, our silences would be sufficient. Our creations and the beauty of our functions would be enough. Our giving would be our perpetual gift.

4

The greatest inspiration, the most sublime ideas of living that have come down to humanity come from a higher realm, a happier realm, a place of pure dreams, a heaven of blessed notions. Ideas and infinite possibilities dwell there in absolute tranquillity.

Before these ideas came to us they were pure, they were silent, and their life-giving possibilities were splendid. But when they come to our earthly realm they acquire weight and words. They become less.

The sweetest notions, ideas of universal love and justice, love for one another, or intuitions of joyful creation, these are all perfect in their heavenly existences. Any artist will tell you that ideas are happier in the heaven of their conception than on the earth of their realisation.

We should return to pure contemplation, to sweet meditation, to the peace of silent loving, the serenity of deep faith, to the stillness of deep waters. We should sit still in our deep selves and dream good new things for humanity. We should try and make those dreams real. We should keep trying to raise higher the conditions and possibilities of this world. Then maybe one day, after much striving, we might well begin to create a world justice and a new light on this earth that could inspire a ten-second silence of wonder – even in heaven.

AMONGST THE
SILENT STONES

When I read Herodotus and when I look at some Renaissance paintings, I find myself uncovering some of the lies that have been told us in history books. When I look at the bronze representations of Portuguese soldiers from the Benin Kingdom, it occurs to me that history is essentially silent. It is we, looking back with clear eyes, who can make it speak. This is our privilege.

In Renaissance paintings I sometimes see that the interaction between Europe and Africa is an old one. The relationship wasn't necessarily coded with notions of degradation. That came later, to an age degraded with notions of conquest. In African sculptings of Europeans I notice that the white visitants were *not* seen as gods but as men, human in their squat representative forms, their helmets, and guns.

The true possibilities of the interactions between people haven't yet begun. This is evident in modern art, in the paintings of Picasso and the Cubists who saw only the outward forms of African Art. The Surrealists saw only the insurgent subconscious content, the world of dreams, the perception that our relationship to the cosmos can only be on human terms, and that we represent and harness the great forces through those strange forms that well up from the depths of the human psyche. They did not begin to see the spiritual life, the mythic structures, the incantatory world-view, and the secret histories that shaped the African's artistic genius.

The beautiful thing about even the most superficial attempt to collide with the secret lives of others is what can only be termed the aesthetic of serendipity: the accidental discoveries, the widened horizons, roads opened by lightning flash into the forests of reality.

The Cubists pursued one aspect of the discoveries made from African art. It led to the breaking up of form. It also led to the belief in four dimensions. The Surrealists delved into the subconscious, and swam on the surface of the oceanic possibilities of what was really the Shaman's terrain. For Shamans and African image-makers know that we contain the universe inside us, that the sea is in the fish much as the fish is in the sea; that birds breathe their own flight; that forces in the human frame can interpenetrate matter, extend the bounds of time and space, enter the dreams of lions, and travel through the private histories of rivers and mountains.

It is a bewildering fact that while we launch out to distant planets, while we approach the wonder and dread of a new millennium (one that could see the human race bring about its own extinction, or enter the greatest stage of its development), as human beings we have not yet begun to *see* one another as people who are forced to be together must. Human history is hundreds of thousands of years old and still we look at one another with superficial eyes – as if we haven't learnt in all these millennia of interacting that we are all merely human, that beneath our skins there are continents of similar desires and eruptive dreams, swirling universes of thoughts, pre-historic urges, lightning flashes, and an eternal bloom of flowers.

It is bewildering because it seems that beneath the strife of our age, internecine warfare, tribal antagonisms, religious intolerance, racial violence, the disharmony of the sexes, beneath all these lurks the most ordinary discovery that we are human, and that life is holy.

We have not yet discovered what it means to be human. And it seems that this *ordinary* discovery is the most epiphanic that can be made – for when we have learnt what it is to be human, when we have *suffered* it, and loved it, we will know our true estate, we will know what gulf separates us from the gods, we will know what it means to be free, and we will know that freedom is really the *beginning* of our mutual destinies.

The Cubists were excited by the fourth dimension in art. The African sculptors bore testament to a fifth dimension, a world of spirits, the interpenetration of the worlds of the living and the dead. Those who forget death forget how to live. The African world, by opening life into death, by drawing death over the living spaces, gave life more space in which to live, to celebrate, to bear suffering, and to be joyful.

Many discoveries have been interrupted by history, discoveries which could lead to fundamental principles that would annihilate all the superficial distinctions of skin, religion, class and sex, by which we conduct our lives. Europe interrupted some of the mythic dreams and the psychic discoveries of places like Africa and India, and then denied the existence of their unique ways. It wasn't always like that: for a time these places fascinated Europe with their deep mysteries. The colonisation of Africa, and its subsequent representation, apart from being the triumph of greed over humanity, was the triumph of rationalism over the subconscious, the victory of the head over the spirit. That triumph, as any psycho-analyst would confirm, is short-lived, and ultimately disastrous. The dreams of the world are more insurgent when repressed.

Apart from the wounding of the souls of continents, colonialism also – paradoxically – achieved an accidental serendipity. It brought people together in a way that might not have happened for hundreds of years. For example, as a result of its over-reaching, Britain began by colonising half the world and now finds half the world in its territory, within its history, subtly altering its psyche. Things work both ways. It is interesting to hear some people complain about these presences living in the land, to hear statements about retaining the purity of the race. The fact is that in nature all organic things of single strain have short histories. Obsessions about purity of blood have wiped out empires. We are all of us mixtures, and our roots are fed from diverse and forgotten places. The Yorubas of Nigeria trace their origins to the Middle East; some anthropologists claim that the real aborigines of Africa are the Bushmen of the Kalahari; the English are a combination of Celts, Vikings, Brigantes, and so on; the ancient Egyptians were black as well as dun-coloured. This is the history of bodies. The history of civilisations is even more eclectic.

We are on the threshold of a new era. The greatest responsibilities of our age rest not only with the big nation powers of the modern world, but also with the host of small nations, those whose ancient dreams are on the verge of extinction. The responsibilities of the unvalued, the unheard, the silent, are greater than ever. And the weight of this responsibility rests on one thing: we are essentially struggling for the humanity of the world. We are struggling to liberate the world into a greater destiny. We are struggling for world balance and justice.

The unheard have always seen themselves as strangers in a world of juggernauts. We have accepted the world's definition of us. The world is neutral: it is we who give things value. We could change the value we place on ourselves. We should always remember that it takes a certain natural genius to survive the depredations of history. We should reconnect that genius, for if we do not place the highest value on ourselves we cannot achieve the highest good in the world.

And, whether we like it or not, what happens in the world is our responsibility as well. The world is a battleground of mythologies and of dreams. Those who allow their houses to fall into chaos and disarray deserve to have the silences of forgotten histories wash over them. As the thunderous roll of world powers gets larger, more silences are created. Those who have lived with nature, those who have suffered the erosion of unexplored paths of history, cannot afford to be silent, to be cowardly, and to think only of themselves.

The new theory of chaos asserts that the flutter of a butterfly's wings can start, can herald, momentous storms. The same may be true of history. The dying star of a nation, the silent death of a language, the eclipse of a way of seeing, the definite cry of a silenced people, could herald something more momentous than a storm for human history.

It is not the size of the voice that is important: it is the power, the truth, and the beauty of the dream.

Those who think that the homogenising forces of the world will not turn their valued spaces into little deserts without mystery deserve to see the coming of the storm. Those who watch in opportunistic silence the growth of tyranny, the swelling ranks of conformity, the rankling prisons, the cracking down of dissent, and the curious new methods of censorship, deserve to witness the world become smaller, tightening around their throats.

Tyranny takes many forms, but all the forms have something in common: a homogenising advance, a fertile bed of discontent and silence. It seems to me that the age demands that each man and woman become a light, a fire, a responsible heir to all the veins of freedom and courage that have enabled us all to get here, in spite of the forces of darkness all around. It seems our age demands that we all be clearer about ourselves than ever, that we be stronger, more courageous in the defence of a multiplicity of voices.

They tell me that nature is a survival of the fittest. And yet look at how many wondrous gold and yellow fishes prosper amongst the silent stones of the ocean beds, while sharks eternally prowl the waters in their impossible dreams of oceanic domination and while whales become extinct; look how many does and ante-lopes, ants and fleas, birds of aquamarine plumage, birds that have mastered Chinua Achebe's art of flying without perching, how many butterflies and iguanas thrive, while elephants turn into endangered species, and while even lions growl in their dwindling solitude.

There is no such thing as a powerless people. There are only those who have not seen and have not used their power and will. It would seem a miraculous feat, but it is possible for the unvalued ones to help create a beautiful new era in human history. New vision should come from those who suffer most and who love life the most. The marvellous responsibility of the unheard and the unseen resides in this paradox.

Nature and history are not just about the survival of the fittest, but also about the survival of the wisest, the most adaptive, and the most aware.

FABLES ARE MADE OF THIS:
FOR KEN SARO-WIWA
(1941–96)

If you want to know what is happening in an age or in a nation, find out what is happening to the writers, the town-criers; for they are the seismographs that calibrate impending earthquakes in the spirit of the times. Are the writers sleeping? Then the age is in a dream. Are the writers celebrating? Then the first flowers of a modest golden age are sending their fragrances across to the shores of future possibilities. Are the writers strangely silent? Then the era is brooding with undeciphered disturbances. But when you hear that writers have been inexplicably murdered, silenced, that their houses have mysteriously burnt down, that grotesque lies are told against them, that they have fled their countries, that they dwell restlessly in exile, but above all when you hear that writers have been sentenced to death by unjust tribunals, then you can be sure that perils and the demons of war and the angels of fragmentation have already begun their dreaded descent into the blood and the suffering of the millions of people who inhabit that land.

Then you know that the air of that land is already rich with corruption and terror, that the air is unbreathable, that the lives are insufferable, that the soil has already begun to deliver its harvest of dead bodies and the bizarre plants of disaster, that liberty is dead in the fields, and that the government itself is under the grim sentence of death.

The writer is the barometer of the age. Elections can be rigged, their results undemocratically annulled, and the rightful leaders installed in the presidential quarters of prison houses. The people can be frightened into sullen acceptance, into cynicism, for the sake of their children, for the sake of food. And they can go on living, blessed by their incredible ability to wait for the diseased time to consume itself, for better seasons to return, and for the earth to decompose the arrogant certainties of tyrants.

But the writer, bristling with the unacceptable that grows swollen in their sleeplessness, unable to carry on for the sheer smell of dung in the age, the writer cannot help but break cover from the wisdom of waiting, cannot help but break faith temporarily with the wisdom of the people who have seen so many monstrosities come and go, so many famines consume themselves to death, so many wars devour their children and eventually expire in a landscape devastated and deserted.

The writer breaks cover; the writer cries out at what the oil companies are doing to the earth, the destruction of the land; the writer cries out at the injustices that run over and now spill out in floods across the streets and byways; the writer wails words of blood at the death of democracy, the beginning of fragmentation and civil war; the writer sometimes even abandons the pen out of monumental frustration, and takes other routes to warn and draw attention to what can no longer be accepted – they become activists, they become soldiers, or they take to politics as an extension of their loving rage.

For, essentially, it is love that we are talking about here; love for the better life that could be real for all the people; love for the greater possibilities of the future that are being murdered in the present by short-sighted leaders; love for the greater way, a higher justice that sits in the land like a wise and invisible god; love for better breathing in the beggar and the basket-weaver; love for women who bear all the suffering and wend their ways to deserted marketplaces and who create such small miracles of survival out of the bitter dust of the dying age; love for the children who grow up under a generous sun and who do not know just how distorted and blood-ridden are the futures they will inherit, who play in the streets and at their games while poison and despair gather about them and hover over their heads like the angels of death; love for the regeneration of a people who deserve so much better and who never seem to get any justice or many good days or much hope on this round earth which glows like a miraculous dream in space to the astonished gaze of astronauts.

It is love for mankind's better future, desire that we may all be better, that our mistakes be higher ones and that the lowest level in living conditions be at least one which is adequate; it is love that drives the seed into becoming the future tree; it is love that makes people extend their hands across seas, across race, across creeds, forging links that make the human dream grow into splendid human realities; it is love that drives the mother to protect the child against suffering; it is love that makes the writer weep when a bloodtide announces itself just over the horizon.

And when this love has been sentenced to death, then those who have hearts that beat with blood, those with flesh that feels the wind and the caress of a lover and life's infinitely graded sufferings, anyone who feels life within should hear this cry – writers are being sentenced to death, sentenced for trying to draw attention to what is being done to the land in the name of profit, and executed for trying to remind a nation, in their own way, of something that should be an acknowledged law that governs the rise and fall of nations and peoples: what does not grow, dies; what does not face its truth, perishes; those without vision deserve the destruction that will fall upon them; those who believe that they can suppress freedom and yet live in freedom are hopelessly deluded. Either a nation faces its uncomfortable truths, or it is overwhelmed by them; for there is a prophetic consequence in the perpetuation of lies, just as there is an unavoidable fate for all those who refuse to see.

There are some things on earth that are stronger than death. One of these is the eternal human quest for justice; a people cannot live without it, and in due course they will be prepared to die to make it possible for their children.

Fables are made of this.

THE JOYS OF

STORYTELLING III

Aphorisms and Fragments

I

To poison a nation, poison its stories. A demoralised nation tells demoralised stories to itself. Beware of the storytellers who are not fully conscious of the importance of their gifts, and who are irresponsible in the application of their art: they could unwittingly help along the psychic destruction of their people.

2

The parables of Jesus are more powerful and persuasive than his miracles.

3

Stories are as ubiquitous as water or air, and as essential. There is not a single person who is not touched by the silent presence of stories.

4

A people are as healthy and confident as the stories they tell themselves. Sick storytellers can make their nations sick. And sick nations make for sick storytellers.

5

Great leaders understand the power of the stories they project to their people. They understand that stories can change an age, turn an era round.

6

Great eras are eras in which great stories are lived and told.

7

Great leaders tell their nations fictions that alter their perceptions. Napoleon exemplified this, and made himself into an enthralling story. Even bad leaders know the power of negative stories.

8

All the great religions, all the great prophets, found it necessary to spread their message through stories, fables, parables. The Bible is one of the world's greatest fountains of fiction and dream.

9

The miracles of Jesus came down to us as stories, magical stories. It is the stories, rather than the facts, which still enchant us towards belief.

10

Alexander the Great conquered all of the known world. But Alexander himself was gently conquered by Homer.

11

Without fighting, stories have won over more people than all the great wars put together.

12

The greatest religions convert the world through stories.

13

A great challenge for our age, and future ages: to do for storytelling what Joyce did for language – to take it to the highest levels of enchantment and magic; to impact into story infinite richness and convergences; to make story flow with serenity, with eternity.

14

Stories are the secret reservoir of values: change the stories individuals or nations live by and tell themselves, and you change the individuals and nations.

15

Nations and peoples are largely the stories they feed themselves. If they tell themselves stories that are lies, they will suffer the future consequences of those lies. If they tell themselves stories that face their own truths, they will free their histories for future flowerings.

16

There is a natural justice to the incontrovertible logic of the way stories reveal their hidden selves.

17

Stories are either dangerous or liberating because they are a kind of destiny.

18

The fact of storytelling hints at a fundamental human unease, hints at human imperfection. Where there is perfection there is no story to tell.

19

In the beginning there were no stories.

20

That previous fragment is a story.

21

The universe began as a story.

22

When we have made an experience or a chaos into a story we have transformed it, made sense of it, transmuted experience, domesticated the chaos.

23

When we started telling stories we gave our lives a new dimension: the dimension of meaning – apprehension – comprehension.

24

Only those who have lived, suffered, thought deeply, loved profoundly, known joy and the tragic penumbra of things tell truly wonderful stories.

25

Stories do not belong to eternity. They belong to time. And out of time they grow. And it is through lives that touch the bedrock of suffering and the fire of the soul, it is through lives, and in time, that stories – relived and redreamed – become timeless.

26

The greatest stories are those that resonate our beginnings and intuit our endings (our mysterious origins and our numinous destinies), and dissolve them both into one.

27

Homo fabula: we are storytelling beings.

28

We are part human, part stories.

29

It is through the fictions and stories we tell ourselves and others that we live the life, hide from it, harmonise it, canalise it, have a relationship with it, shape it, accept it, are broken by it, redeem it, or flow with the life.

30

Without stories we would go mad. Life would lose its moorings or lose its orientations. Even in silence we are living out stories.

31

Stories can drive you mad.

32

Stories can heal profound sicknesses of the spirit.

33

It is through their stories that the ancient Greeks so profoundly influence and shape the world. Prometheus, Ixion, Sisyphus, Perseus, the Gorgon's head, Calypso, Odysseus – their stories are eternal metaphors of the partially revealed nature of the human condition.

34

Africa breathes stories.

35

In Africa everything is a story, everything is a repository of stories. Spiders, the wind, a leaf, a tree, the moon, silence, a glance, a mysterious old man, an owl at midnight, a sign, a white stone on a branch, a single yellow bird of omen, an inexplicable death, an unprompted laughter, an egg by the river, are all impregnated with stories. In Africa things are stories, they store stories, and they yield stories at the right moment of dreaming, when we are open to the secret side of objects and moods.

36

Africa is a land bristling with too many stories and moods. This over-abundance of stories, this pollulation, is a sort of chaos. A land of too many stories is a land that doesn't necessarily learn from its stories. It should trade some of its stories for clarity. Stories hint both at failure and celebration. Dying lands breed stories in the air like corpses breed worms. A land beginning to define itself, to create beauty and order from its own chaos, moves from having too many moods and stories in the air to having clear structures, silences, clear music, muted and measured celebrations, lucid breezes, freed breathing, tentative joys, the limpid freshness of new dawns over places sighted across the sea for the first time. If suffering breeds stories, then the transformation of suffering into a higher order and beauty and func-tionality breathes tranquillity.

37

Tranquillity is the resolution of the tensions and paradoxes of story into something beyond story: into stillness.

38

Unhappy lands prefer utopian stories.

Happy lands prefer unhappy stories.

39

The stories of the Egyptians and the Greeks, rather than their poems, shaped the world's consciousness and named the stars.

40

For Africans the world is imbued with stories, legends, tales.

41

The African mind is essentially abstract, and their storytelling is essentially philosophical.

42

The happiness of Africa is in its nostalgia for the future, and its dreams of a golden age.

43

In Africa the mood in its music is a poignant golden story of everlasting hope and prayer.

44

Where stories are, struggles have been lived through, fates have been lived out, triumphs have danced with failures, and human destinies have left their imprints and their souls and their stories on the land, in the air, and even on the waters. Strangers to these lands can feel the vibrations of the people's forgotten histories and fates in the air.

45

Moods are stories unspoken, condensed in the air, untold. Stories become moods, and are moods unfurled, allowed to grow.

46

The transparency of excellent stories: words dissolve words, and only things stand in their place.

47

In bad stories words cancel themselves out, and nothing is left. The words return to their source; they desert the page; only meaningless marks are left behind.

48

Story is paradox.

49

The superiority of one writer over another is not just in the quality of language; but also in the quality of the story and the storytelling; the quality of enchantment; and the timelessness of that enchantment. It is therefore futile to speak of superiorities. There is only that which lives, and which keeps on living.

———

50

Creating the smallest living thing, creating life, no matter how small, is greater than creating a vast dead planet. A thing that lives is a universe.

51

It is in the creation of story, the lifting of story into the realms of art, it is in this that the higher realms of creativity reside.

52

A good story keeps on growing. A good story never dies.

53

Stories are the wisest surviving parts of a people's stupidities or failings.

54

A people without stories would be a perfected people or a forgetful people, or an insane people – which is to say that they are a mythical people, or have ceased to exist, or are on their way to doing so.

55

Stories can destroy civilisations, can win wars, can lose them, can conquer hearts by the millions, can transform enemies into friends, can help the sick towards healing, can sow the seeds of the creation of empires, can undo them, can reshape the psychic mould of a people, can remould the political and spiritual temper of an age.

56
Stories can be either bacteria or light: they can infect a system, or illuminate a world.

57
Like water, stories are much taken for granted. They are seemingly ordinary and neutral, but are one of humanity's most powerful weapons for good or evil.

58
It is easy to forget how mysterious and mighty stories are. They do their work in silence, invisibly. They work with all the internal materials of the mind and self. They become part of you while changing you. Beware the stories you read or tell: subtly, at night, beneath the waters of consciousness, they are altering your world.

59
Stories are one of the highest and most invisible forms of human creativity.

60

Stories are always a form of resistance.

61

There is a perpetual creativity involved in storytelling. Stories make people more creative, negatively or positively.

62

The writing of stories: the hidden frame, the hidden harmony.

63

The miracle of stories, and the mystery.

64

The storytelling quality in Mozart's music. How certain bars, certain notes in the Piano Concerto 27 hint at a story that goes something like this: 'One day, when I was happy, a nightingale flew past my window, and the love of my life left me for another.'

65

Music and stories: the notes that haunt us because they have become the moods of our joys and our sweet sadnesses for ever.

66

The grief of Orpheus is a story told with anguish over and over again, every day, for seven years, and told in all its agonising internal permutations.

67

Orpheus's grief is the mother of music, but is itself born of story, a story unbearable to live, obsessive to tell – the story of our inescapable loss, and the measure of our love.

68

The infinite interpretability of great stories – and their serenity.

69

To see the madness and yet walk a perfect silver line.

70

The greatest guide is the clearest spirit and mind.

71

That's what the true storyteller should be: a great guide, a clear mind, who can walk a silver line in hell or madness. Dante chose Virgil. I would choose Jesus, or the Buddha, or Lao Tsu, or Homer.

72

Great storytellers seldom found religions. Great founders of religions are always excellent storytellers.

73

Only a profound storyteller would say something like: 'Suffer the little children to come unto me.'

74

The great essays on storytelling are done in stories themselves.

75

The true storyteller suffers the chaos and the madness, the nightmare – resolves it all, sees clearly, and guides you surely through the fragmentation and the shifting world.

76

I am not referring to just any story, but only to those great ones, rich and rare, that haunt, that elude, that tantalise, that have the effect of poignant melodies lodged deep in barely reachable places of the spirit. The human race is not blessed with many stories of this quality.

77

The magician and the evangelist have much in common: both have to distract (our attention).

78

The magician and the politician also have much in common: they both have to draw our attention away from what they are really doing.

79

Magic distracts our attention from the hidden methods, art draws our attention to the hidden revelation.

80

Magic becomes art when it has nothing to hide.

81

The higher the artist, the fewer the gestures.

82

The fewer the tools, the greater the imagination.

83

The greater the will, the greater the secret failure.

84

It is precisely in a broken age that we need mystery and a reawakened sense of wonder: need them in order to be whole again.

85

Philosophy is most powerful when it resolves into story. But story is amplified in power by the presence of philosophy.

86

The infinite life of a beautiful story.

87

Creativity is a secular infinity.

88

Creativity is evidence of the transhuman.

89

Creativity is the highest civilising faculty.

90

Love is the greatest creativity of them all, and the most blessed.

91

Creativity of any valuable kind is one of the fullest expressions of the human and the godlike within us.

92

The greatest joy is that of love — loving life, loving others, loving yourself, loving your work. The next greatest joy is the freedom to serve.

93

Creativity is love, a very high kind of love.

94

The imagination is one of the highest gifts we have.

95

To find life in myth, and myth in life.

96

Maybe there are only three kinds of stories: the stories we live, the stories we tell, and the higher stories that help our souls fly up towards the greater light.

97

All great stories are enigmas.

98
Humility is the watchword at creativity's gate.

99
Creativity is a form of prayer, and the expression of a profound gratitude for being alive.

100
Ah, the sweet suffering of creativity.

101
Politics is the art of the possible; creativity is the art of the impossible.

REDREAMING THE WORLD

For Chinua Achebe

The ancient Romans built straight roads wherever they went. Christians planted churches on resistant landscapes. Muslims pierce the air with the call of the muezzin.

Conquerors are transplanters. So are the conquered and exiles. They take their earth with them, carry with them their rituals as codes of continuity in the new world. But the oppressed always find themselves in paradoxical waters that both show up their presence and render them invisible.

Those who dream of dominating the world should expect the world to overrun them. To impose your will on another is to surrender the right to your own space. To swallow the history of others into your own history is to expect to be constipated with the history of others.

In their over-reaching, colonisers always become transparent. Their language hides nothing. The oppressed always understand what is being said. World-dominators have no secret language in which to hide. The oppressed retain the moods of their languages. They are always opaque.

The oppressors become so inflated with their history, their apparent stability, and their military power that they forget how to listen to and how to see others. In the face of inscrutable time, they seem to flourish in this hubris. They forget that the world is one, and that the fates of oppressed and oppressor are bound up with one another for ever.

The future of all is jeopardised by the egotism of contemporary victors.

The oppressed always live with death. They die in life. Suffering drenches them in mystery. Intense experiences accelerate their ageing. They mature more strangely and more deeply than their oppressors. And yet they often think of their victors as their standard of aspiration. Lack of historical confidence leads them into this bifurcation of thinking. They have not as a people learnt how to snatch historical confidence from the most unlikely places, from the fact that they are still here on this planet, inhabiting some sort of space, that they often survived slavery and all manner of outrages, drought, famine, dictatorships, bad governments, bitter wars, mass imprisonments and other permutations of human viciousness. They many be dwindling but it is precisely because of all they have suffered and are still suffering that they have much to struggle for, to be alive for, beyond the mountains of their crisis.

The dreams of the oppressed are planted in the earth and watered through all the bitter seasons. Their suffering could make them farmers of dreams. Their harvest could make the world more just and more beautiful. It is only the oppressed who have this sort of difficult and paradoxical potential.

It is an enigma. Those who suffer are always in that place that binds roots to the earth. They are also always in exile. Suffering is their centre, their heart. It reminds them of who they are. The oppressed live within the stomach of their oppressors. They need the thinking and the structure of their oppressors to transform their realities. The oppressors need the blood of the oppressed for the rejuvenation of their spirits. The spirits of all become weirder.

It would seem that the oppressor is the challenge of the oppressed. It would seem that the oppressed have to accept the standards of their age, have to meet them, and raise them higher, add their genius to the universal dream. It would appear that they have to compete in this world, but not necessarily on the sullied terms of the world dominators. They have to fight for their places in the modern proscenium. They can no longer, it would seem, hold themselves down with rage about their historical past or their intolerable present. But they have to find the humility and the silence to transcend their rage, distill it into the highest creativity and use it to reveal greater truths.

They have to regroup their powers and build again from the wedding of the best things the world has to offer and the best aspects of their own mythic, aesthetic, spiritual, and scientific frames. They mustn't forget that distance and their sufferings help them to see better what sort of future they want to create. With humility and with passion they could learn from the world and teach the world to learn from them. Along the way it is necessary to clear the cobwebs of bewilderment from their eyes, and to demystify the propaganda of the contemporary victors.

The contemporary victors in the abundance of their economic constellation are also spinning in a curious stasis of spiritual and cultural life. They have forgotten death. They are blind to the monsters of unresolved history lurking in the cellars of their modern dreams. They have forgotten the inescapable inter-connectedness of all things. In arrogating to themselves the centre of the world, when in fact the centre is everywhere, the contemporary victors are speaking to the universe on behalf of everyone and speaking badly. It is time now for them to listen, and to listen the way human beings have never listened before. It is time to listen to the speech of poisoned dolphins, the cries of the stratosphere, the howls of the deforestated earth, the caterwauling of the dry winds over the encroaching deserts, the screams of people without hope and without food, to the silences of strangled nations, to the passionate dreams of difficult artists, and to the age-old warnings that have always lurked in the oral fables of storytellers and shamans.

It should no longer be left to the contemporary victors to speak for human history. Whatever resilience has kept wounded people and devastated continents here, alive, can be transfigured to make them strong, confident, and serene. They have to question everything, in order to rebuild for the future. They have to redream the world. Chinua Achebe put it very succinctly when he wrote that suffering could also give rise to something beautiful.

It is possible that a sense of beauty, of justice, of the inter-connectedness of all things, may yet save the human species from self-annihilation. We are all still learning how to be free. Freedom is the beginning of the greatest possibilities of the human genius. It is not the goal.

———

★

The real quarrel of the oppressed is not with the oppressors. It is with themselves. The real truth they have to face is the truth about themselves. Hope and striving have magic in them. Those who have much to strive for, much to resolve and overcome and redream, may well be luckier than they think. Struggle is life. And there is something awesomely beautiful and history-making about those who have set out to climb the seven mountains of their predicaments, towards the new destinies that lie beyond, with the star of hope above their heads.

For in their patience and in their egalitarian triumph they can teach us all how to live again and how to love again and could well make it possible for us all to create the beginnings of the first truly universal civilisation in the history of recorded and unrecorded time.